Clever Crafting *with* FLEA MARKET FINDS

*W*hether you've been cleaning out the attic or browsing a
favorite flea market, you're all set to join in the excitement of
reviving those seemingly useless "finds" into magnificent crafts!
From unique home décor to exceptional handmade gifts, we've
gathered over 85 fun projects that make great use of "treasures"
found in unlikely places. This volume features innovative ideas for
transforming discards into wonderful home accessories, creative
showcases for your decorations, and fabulous furnishings.
No matter how little time or skill you have, you're sure
to find the perfect project as you turn the pages
of this clever collection. Enjoy!

LEISURE ARTS, INC.
Little Rock, Arkansas

Clever Crafting with FLEA MARKET FINDS

EDITORIAL STAFF

Vice President and Editor-at-Large: Anne Van Wagner Childs
Vice President and Editor-in-Chief: Sandra Graham Case
Director of Designer Relations: Debra Nettles
Publications Director: Kristine Anderson Mertes
Design Director: Cyndi Hansen
Special Projects Director: Patricia A. Sowers
Editorial Director: Susan Frantz Wiles
Creative Art Director: Gloria Bearden
Photography Director: Karen Hall
Art Operations Director: Jeff Curtis

DESIGN
Senior Designers: Diana Sanders Cates and
  Cherece Athy Cooper
Designers: Polly Tullis Browning, Peggy Elliot Cunningham,
  Anne Pulliam Stocks, Linda Diehl Tiano, and Becky Werle
Executive Assistant: Debra Smith

TECHNICAL
Managing Editor: Leslie Schick Gorrell
Senior Technical Writer: Theresa Hicks Young
Technical Writer: Sherry Solida Ford
Copy Editor: Kimberly J. Smith
Technical Associates: Jennifer Potts Hutchings and
  Jane Kenner Prather

EDITORIAL
Managing Editor: Suzie Puckett
Senior Associate Editor: Jennifer L. Riley
Contributing Editors: Nancy Dockter, Darla Burdette Kelsay,
  and Stacey Robertson Marshall

ART
Art Director: Mark Hawkins
Production Artist: Elaine Barry
Color Technician: Mark R. Potter
Photography Stylists: Tiffany Huffman and Janna Laughlin
Staff Photographer: Russell Ganser
Publishing Systems Administrator: Becky Riddle
Publishing Systems Assistants: Myra S. Means and
  Chris Wertenberger

PROMOTIONS
Associate Editor: Steven M. Cooper
Designer: Dale Rowett
Graphic Artist: Deborah Kelly

BUSINESS STAFF

Publisher: Rick Barton
Vice President, Finance: Tom Siebenmorgen
Director of Corporate Planning and Development:
  Laticia Mull Cornett
Vice President, Retail Marketing: Bob Humphrey
Vice President, Sales: Ray Shelgosh

Vice President, National Accounts: Pam Stebbins
Retail Marketing Director: Margaret Sweetin
Vice President, Operations: Jim Dittrich
Comptroller, Operations: Rob Thieme
Retail Customer Service Manager: Wanda Price
Print Production Manager: Fred F. Pruss

Hardcover ISBN 1-57486-214-6

10 9 8 7 6 5 4 3 2 1

Table of Contents

ACCESSORIES WITH FLAIR 6

Table of Contents

Table of Contents

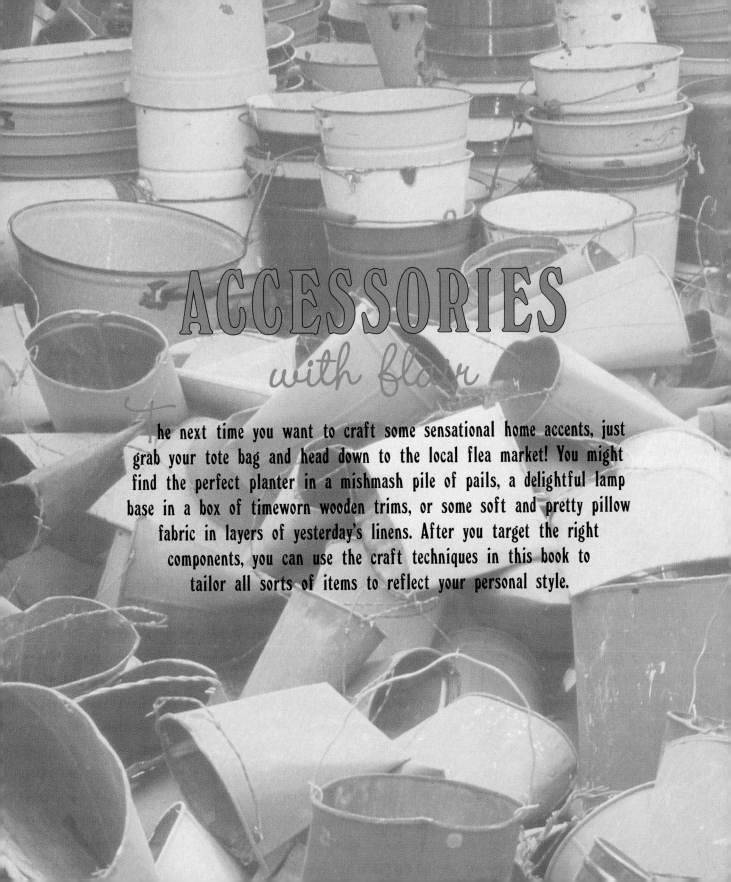

ACCESSORIES
with flair

The next time you want to craft some sensational home accents, just grab your tote bag and head down to the local flea market! You might find the perfect planter in a mishmash pile of pails, a delightful lamp base in a box of timeworn wooden trims, or some soft and pretty pillow fabric in layers of yesterday's linens. After you target the right components, you can use the craft techniques in this book to tailor all sorts of items to reflect your personal style.

FLORAL TEAPOT LAMP

Delightfully charming, a castoff teapot becomes a warm and inviting tabletop lamp. Painted cutouts sculpt the teapot's "lid," and a wooden plate, trimmed with dainty florals, rests on knobs to create the pot's matching "saucer" base. Fabric strips cut with pinking shears give the lampshade a whimsical touch that's just our cup of tea!

FLORAL TEAPOT LAMP

You will need a teapot without a lid (we used a $6^{1}/_{2}$" tall teapot), wood glue, round wooden cutout to fit in opening of teapot, round decorative wooden cutout $^{1}/_{2}$" larger than opening of teapot, 2" dia. round wooden cutout, four $^{1}/_{2}$" dia. wooden knobs, 9" dia. wooden plate, 2 lock nuts, household cement, drill and drill bits, spray primer, acrylic paint in colors to match teapot, paintbrushes, 2 brass washers, 10" pipe stem with threaded ends, lamp socket assembly with cord, self-adhesive lampshade, fabric, pinking shears, fabric glue, and $^{1}/_{2}$"w gimp trim.

Use wood glue for all gluing unless otherwise indicated. Allow wood glue, cement, primer, and paint to dry after each application.

1. For top, center and glue 2" dia. cutout on top of decorative cutout and remaining cutout on bottom of decorative cutout.

2. For base, glue knobs to bottom of plate for feet. Drill a hole to fit lock nut through center of base. Use household cement to glue lock nut in hole flush with top of plate.

3. Drill a $^{3}/_{8}$" dia. hole through center of top, and bottom of teapot.

4. Apply primer, then two coats of paint to top and base. Paint designs on base to match teapot.

5. Place remaining lock nut, then one washer on one end of pipe stem; secure in base. Place teapot, then top on pipe stem; use household cement to glue top to teapot. Place remaining washer on pipe stem.

6. Twist socket base onto top of pipe. Loosen screws on socket. Thread cord up through pipe. Wrap one wire on cord around one screw on socket; tighten screw. Repeat to attach remaining wire to opposite side. Snap socket shell into socket base.

7. Follow manufacturer's instructions to cover lampshade with fabric. Use pinking shears to cut 1"w fabric strips $^{1}/_{4}$" shorter than height of shade and one strip to fit around bottom of shade. Spacing evenly, use fabric glue to attach short strips on shade; glue remaining strip around bottom of shade. Overlapping ends at back, use fabric glue to attach trim around top and bottom of shade.

LAMP DIAGRAM

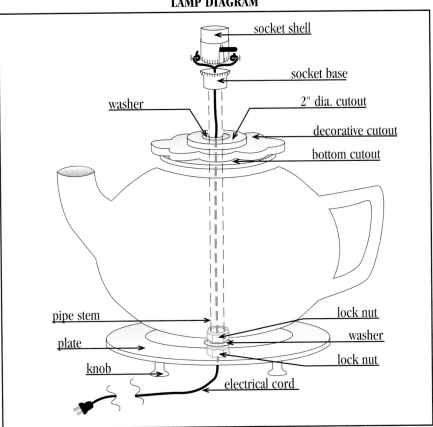

socket shell
socket base
washer
2" dia. cutout
decorative cutout
bottom cutout
pipe stem
lock nut
washer
lock nut
plate
knob
electrical cord

"GRATE" NIGHT-LIGHT

*C*ook up this "grate" night-light and stop stumbling around in the dark! Simply decorate an old grater with a string of antique and crystal beads. Replace the plastic cover of an ordinary night-light with your clever creation. You'll be "de-light-ed" with the sparkling results!

GRATER NIGHT-LIGHT

You will need clear acrylic spray sealer, small half-round metal grater, assorted beads, gold craft wire, wire cutters, night-light without automatic sensor, and household cement.

1. Apply two coats of sealer to grater and allow to dry.

2. For each line of beads, thread end of wire through one hole in grater from front to back; twist end to form a knot that will not pull through hole. Thread beads onto wire as desired, then insert end of wire from front to back through a hole on opposite edge of grater; knot and trim wire end.

3. Leaving switch exposed, glue grater to night-light.

WILD WALL DÉCOR

*A*nswer the call of the wild with exotic artwork to decorate your walls! Pick up old metal trays at a rummage sale or flea market and revive them by sponge painting and applying finger-painted "leopard spots." Add animal pictures and ribbon hangers for a unique addition to your favorite room.

ANIMAL PRINT TRAYS

For each tray, you will need a metal tray; spray primer; yellow, brown, dark brown, and black acrylic paint; foam brushes; painter's masking tape; natural sponge; gold paint pen; animal motif picture; decorative-edge craft scissors; spray adhesive; clear acrylic spray sealer; 1 yd. of 1¹/₂"w satin ribbon; and a hot glue gun.

Refer to Painting Techniques, page 123, before beginning project. Allow primer, paint, and sealer to dry after each application.

1. Clean tray and allow to dry; apply primer.

2. Paint bottom of tray black, then rim yellow.

3. Mask ends of tray bottom. *Sponge Paint* center section brown; lightly sponge rim brown. Remove tape.

4. For spots, use finger to smear brown and dark brown paint on rim.

5. Use paint pen to outline brown and black sections and paint dots on black areas.

6. Use craft scissors to trim edges of motif. Apply spray adhesive to back of motif and smooth onto center of tray.

7. Apply two coats of sealer to tray.

8. Tie a bow at center of ribbon. Glue streamers to back of tray for hanger.

TASSELED BAUBLES

*I*deal for dressing up the knobs of a china cabinet or armoire, these romantic tasseled adornments are made from common glass drawer pulls, beads, and an assortment of fringe, gimp, and other trims. You'll be amazed at how quickly these decorative baubles open the door to a new look for the entire room!

DRAWER PULL TASSELS
Bullion Fringe Tassel

You will need 1 yd. of gold 20-gauge craft wire, wire cutters, 3³/₄" long straight wooden clothespin, pliers, hot glue gun, 5¹/₂" long bullion fringe, 1¹/₂" long brush fringe, ¹/₂"w decorative gimp trim, glass drawer pull with hole through center, and one each 18mm and 16mm faceted glass beads.

1. For hanger, cut two 18" lengths of wire; twist wires together. Place slit in clothespin over center of twisted wires; bring ends of wires to top of clothespin and twist once to secure.

2. Wrap and glue a length of bullion fringe around bottom of clothespin. Wrap and glue two layers of fringe just above first layer; repeat to add a third layer above second layer.

3. Wrap and glue a length of brush fringe over top of last layer of bullion fringe. Glue gimp trim around head of clothespin. Cut one strand from bullion fringe; beginning with cut end, glue strand around tassel on top of brush fringe.

4. Thread hanger wires through drawer pull, 18mm bead, then 16mm bead. Form wire into a loop; wrap wire ends around loop close to bead; trim ends.

Brush Fringe Tassel

You will need two skeins #5 pearl cotton, one skein embroidery floss, 5" square of cardboard, hot glue gun, 5¹/₂" long brush fringe, ¹/₂"w gimp trim, glass drawer pull with hole through center, 18mm faceted glass bead, and an 8mm glass bead.

1. For hanger, cut four 12" lengths of pearl cotton; place lengths together and set aside. For tassel tie, cut a 6" length of pearl cotton; set aside.

2. For tassel, wrap embroidery floss and remaining pearl cotton together around cardboard. Thread hanger to center under threads at one end of cardboard (Fig. 1); knot hanger tightly around threads. Cut threads at bottom of cardboard. Knot tassel tie around tassel ³/₄" from hanger.

Fig. 1

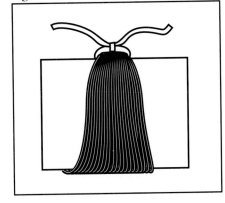

3. Beginning at tassel tie and working toward hanger, glue brush fringe around tassel. Wrap and glue gimp trim around top of fringe.

4. Thread hanger ends through drawer pull, 18mm bead, then 8mm bead. Split hanger threads in half; wrap around, then back up though 8mm bead (Fig. 2). Knot ends of hanger together.

Fig. 2

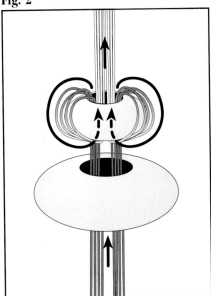

Before vacuum cleaners, there were rug beaters. Relics now, these simple wire tools with interesting shapes nonetheless have a definite folk-art appeal. Showcase them on wall panels of ready-made stretcher bars, covered in burlap. Add a running-stitch border of yarn and big buttons, and you have a display of Americana that anyone will appreciate!

RUG BEATER WALL HANGINGS

For each wall hanging, you will need a staple gun, two 16" and two 28" wooden stretcher strips, burlap, brown yarn, large-eye curved needle, hot glue gun, assorted buttons, and a rug beater.

1. Staple stretcher strips together to make frame.

2. Draw around frame on burlap (wrong side); cut out $2^1/_2$" outside drawn lines. Center frame on wrong side of burlap piece. Folding edges $^1/_2$" to wrong side and pulling burlap taut, staple edges to back of frame.

3. Using yarn and curved needle, work *Running Stitches*, page 122, along edges of wall hanging. Glue buttons along edges.

4. Use yarn to tack rug beater to wall hanging.

RIBBON-WRAPPED FRAME

*B*ring a little romance to your décor with this delicate frame. Simply wrap an old picture frame with satin ribbon and accent it with a bow and faux flowers. Choose a pretty print to display inside, and you've created an adorable accent from someone else's throwaways!

RIBBON-WRAPPED FRAME
You will need corrugated cardboard, desired print, picture frame, spray adhesive, 1½"w wire-edged satin ribbon, hot glue gun, 1½"w sheer ribbon, and a sprig of artificial flowers.

1. Cut cardboard and print to fit frame. Use spray adhesive to attach print to cardboard.

2. Overlapping edges to cover frame completely, wrap satin ribbon around frame; hot glue ends at back of frame to secure. Glue print to back of frame.

3. Using sheer ribbon, follow *Bows*, page 123, to make a bow with six 8" loops and two 4" streamers. Glue bow to top of frame, then flowers to bow.

LOVELY LADDER-BACK SHELF

Freshen up the look of your dressing room or bath with the feminine appeal of this ladder-back shelf. Assembling it from a wooden chair back and a shelf is almost as easy as powdering your nose! A trace-and-paint flower is the crowning touch.

LADDER-BACK SHELF

You will need a saw; wooden ladder-back chair; wooden shelf; drill and bits; two 2" long wood screws; primer; green spray paint; tracing paper; transfer paper; gesso; ivory, light green, green, dark green, tan, and light brown acrylic paint; paintbrushes; and clear acrylic spray sealer.

Refer to Painting Techniques, page 123, before beginning project. Allow gesso, paint, and sealer to dry after each application.

1. Cutting uprights the same length and straight across the bottom, cut back from chair.

2. Center chair back on back edge of shelf. Mark bottom of shelf at center of each upright. Drill a pilot hole through shelf at each mark. Working from bottom of shelf, drive screws through holes into uprights.

3. Apply primer, then two coats of spray paint to chair back and shelf.

4. Trace flower pattern, page 125, onto tracing paper. Use transfer paper to transfer outer lines of design to center of top rung on chair back. Apply gesso inside lines of design. Replace pattern, then transfer all lines of pattern. Paint leaves green with dark green *Shading*

and light green *Highlights*. Paint flower ivory with tan *Shading* and light brown *Linework*. Paint center light brown with ivory outline.

5. Paint bands of color around finials on uprights as desired. Apply two coats of sealer to entire shelf.

SILVERWARE WIND CHIME

*A*fter a quick search through a utensil drawer or flea market box, you'll have everything you need to create a charming wind chime! Simplicity is the key to this fun project — just collect pieces of unmatched silverware and tie them to a fluted metal gelatin mold to make a musical accent for your patio or porch.

SILVERWARE WIND CHIME
You will need a drill and ⅛" bit, assorted pieces of silverware, fluted metal gelatin mold, and silver cord.

1. Drill a hole in handle of each piece of silverware. Spacing holes evenly, drill a hole in bottom of mold for each piece of silverware; drill one hole at center for hanger.

2. Knot ends of an 8" length of cord together to form hanging loop. Thread folded end of loop up through center hole of mold until knot catches.

3. Thread and knot one end of a 12" length of cord through hole in handle of each piece of silverware. Spacing similar pieces opposite each other and adjusting cord lengths for balance, thread cord ends through holes in mold; knot each end to secure.

DAZZLING DRAGONFLY LAMP

*A*ssemble some miscellaneous wood pieces and you're on your way to making this whimsical lamp. For the dazzling globe, apply dragonfly motifs made with liquid leading filled in with colorful glass paint. After adding an electric lamp kit, you've got a wonderful gift to brighten a friend's home.

DRAGONFLY LAMP

You will need freezer paper; liquid leading; clear, green, and tan glass paint; paintbrushes; hurricane globe with 2" dia. base; wood glue; 4" and 5" dia. wooden plaques; 2"h x 2" dia. wooden cup; drill and $^3/_8$" bit; three $^5/_8$" dia. wooden knobs; green and tan acrylic paint; $1^1/_2$" long lamp nipple; candelabra lamp kit; and a 3-watt candelabra bulb.

Allow leading, glass paint, wood glue, and acrylic paint to dry after each application.

1. Using patterns, page 125, draw desired number of dragonflies and circles on dull side of freezer paper. Use leading to draw over each design on shiny side of paper. Use green and tan glass paint to fill in designs.

2. Peel dragonflies and circles from freezer paper and arrange on globe as desired (motifs will adhere to glass). Paint remainder of globe with clear glass paint.

3. For base, center and glue 4" plaque on 5" plaque, then cup on 4" plaque. Drill a $^3/_8$" dia. hole down through center of base. Spacing evenly, glue knobs to bottom of base for feet.

4. Using acrylic paint, paint lamp base green. Paint tan bands around cup; use paintbrush handle to paint dots around base.

5. Thread $^3/_4$" of nipple into hole in base. Follow manufacturer's instructions to assemble lamp kit on base; place globe on base.

19

COMMUNICATIONS CHEST

We polished up this message center by adding corkboard to a timeworn silverware chest. Ideal for the kitchen or home office, the wall-mounted bulletin board folds down to provide a place to keep the paper, pens, and pushpins you'll always need for important communications.

CHEST DIAGRAM

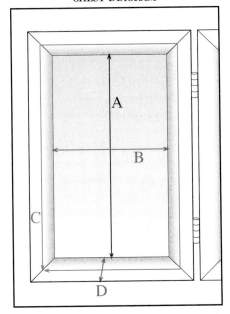

SILVER CHEST MESSAGE CENTER

You will need a wooden silverware chest, sandpaper, tack cloth, clear acrylic spray sealer, fabric, spray adhesive, $\frac{1}{4}$" thick cork, wood glue, miter box and saw, $\frac{5}{8}$"w decorative wooden molding, $\frac{1}{2}$" dia. decorative cord, $\frac{1}{4}$" long wood screws, lightweight chain, wire cutters, magnetic latch, and two sawtooth picture hangers.

Refer to Chest Diagram for all measuring.

1. Remove section dividers and linings from chest.

2. Sand chest; wipe with tack cloth. Apply two coats of sealer to chest; allow to dry.

3. Measure length (A) and width (B) of lid; add $\frac{1}{4}$" to each measurement. Cut a piece from fabric the determined measurements. Apply spray adhesive to wrong side of fabric piece; clipping corners, smooth over inside of lid.

4. Measure around inside edge of lid (C), then measure depth of lid (D); add $\frac{1}{2}$" to each measurement. Cut a strip from fabric the determined measurements; press long edges and one end $\frac{1}{4}$" to wrong side. Apply spray adhesive to wrong side of strip. Beginning with raw end $\frac{1}{4}$" past one corner and matching one long edge to outer edge, adhere fabric strip to inner sides of lid.

5. Repeat Steps 3 and 4 to line inside bottom of chest.

6. Draw around chest on cork; cut out $\frac{3}{4}$" inside drawn line. Center and glue cork on chest lid. Cutting to fit and mitering corners, cut pieces of molding to fit along top edges of cork; glue in place. Allow to dry.

7. Trimming to fit, glue cord along edges of cork; allow to dry.

8. With lid open to a 90° angle and referring to Fig. 1, use screws to attach a length of chain to lid and bottom of chest.

Fig. 1

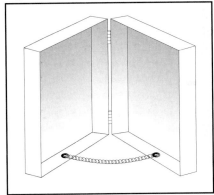

9. To complete message center, follow manufacturer's instructions to attach latch to inside of chest. Attach hangers to back of message center.

ENCHANTING CANDLE BASIN

Brighten your home with the enchanting glow of a tabletop candle basin assembled from a secondhand gelatin mold, a wooden candlestick and plate, and a little paint. Use your favorite shades of crayons to "color" homemade candles to set adrift in the fanciful holder!

GELATIN-MOLD CANDLEHOLDER

You will need household cement; metal gelatin mold; wooden candlestick; wooden plate or plaque for base; white gesso; yellow, blue, and green acrylic paint; paintbrushes; small tart tins to use as candle molds; and floating candle-making kit.

Allow household cement, gesso, paint, and sealer to dry after each application.

1. For candleholder, glue bottom of candlestick to base, then glue gelatin mold to top; allow to dry.

2. Excluding inside of mold, apply gesso, then two coats of yellow paint to candleholder.

3. Paint designs on candleholder as desired.

4. Using tart tins as molds, follow manufacturer's instructions to make candles.

FAUX-SIMPLE STAINED GLASS

*S*earching for the perfect stained glass piece can be time-consuming — and costly. Especially when you can use a castaway window frame to create your own designer accent — inexpensively. Simply outline your pattern on the window with silver liquid leading and fill in the areas with colorful glass paint!

FAUX STAINED GLASS

You will need a washable felt-tip marker, ruler, window, silver liquid leading, and desired colors of glass paint.

1. Use marker and ruler to draw desired design on back of glass.

2. Follow manufacturer's instructions to apply leading over lines on front of glass.

3. Follow manufacturer's instructions to paint window with glass paint.

4. Remove marker lines from back of glass.

NATURE COLLAGE

This tabletop collage is a natural wonder! Painted wooden frames filled with dried naturals stand at attention, attached to another frame that's weighted with pebbles positioned in tile grout. What a great way to display Nature's gifts!

FRAME COLLAGE

You will need four wooden picture frames all the same thickness (we used $^3/_4$" thick frames: one 5" x 7", one 4" square, and two 5" square frames), green acrylic paint, paintbrushes, sandpaper, tack cloth, clear matte acrylic sealer, brown mat board, utility knife, craft glue, hot glue gun, wood screws, two $1^1/_2$" corner brackets, dried naturals (we used flower pods and stems, mushrooms, eucalyptus, corn cobs, and bulbs), cream-colored tile grout, and pebbles.

To determine length of wood screws needed, measure thickness of frames to be joined and subtract $^1/_4$". Use hot glue unless otherwise indicated. Allow paint, sealer, and craft glue to dry after each application.

1. Paint frames green. Lightly sand frames; wipe with tack cloth. Apply two coats of sealer to frames.

2. Draw around frames on wrong side of mat board; cut out just inside drawn lines. Use craft glue to attach right side of mat board pieces to backs of frames.

3. For back, arrange and glue three frames together. Working from back of frames, insert screws where frames overlap to secure.

4. Use corner brackets to attach base frame to back.

5. Arrange and glue dried naturals in back frames; glue pod stems along fronts of frames.

6. Fill base frame with grout to just below top edge; press pebbles into grout and allow to dry.

BREADBOARD BUD VASES

*F*lower an old breadboard with an antique finish and timeless words of budding romance. Use tacks to attach a few bottles with curly wire hangers, then fill the glass vials with fresh daisies for a look you're sure to love!

BREADBOARD BOTTLE VASES

You will need sandpaper, wooden breadboard, tack cloth, green and brown acrylic paint, off-white paint pen, paintbrushes, paste floor wax, clear acrylic spray sealer, small bottles with necks, 19-gauge craft wire, wire cutters, needle-nose pliers, two picture hangers, and ³/₄" long upholstery tacks.

Allow paint and sealer to dry after each application.

1. Lightly sand breadboard; wipe with tack cloth.

2. Paint board brown. Apply a light coat of wax to board; paint board green. Use paint pen to write "He loves me … He loves me not" along edges of board. Lightly sand board for a distressed look; wipe with tack cloth.

3. For wash, mix two parts brown paint with one part water. Working in small sections and immediately using cloth to wipe section, apply wash to board; allow to dry.

4. Apply two coats of sealer to board.

5. For each bottle, cut two 12" lengths of wire. Leaving a 5" tail, twist wires together. Referring to Fig. 1, place bottle between wires, then tightly twist wires together on opposite sides of bottle. Bring one wire from each side to top and twist around each other to form handle. Curl remaining wires at sides of bottle.

Fig. 1

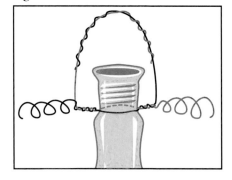

6. Attach hangers to top back of board. Nail tacks to board; hang bottles on tacks.

WILD CANDLESTICK LAMPS

If you've been hunting for a pair of distinctive lamps but haven't found anything you're wild about, set your sights on the classic look of these beaded illuminators. The electrifying duo gets its animal magnetism from pieces of print tissue paper decoupaged to the bases.

VINTAGE BOBBIN LAMPS

For each lamp, you will need a drill and ½" dia. bit, 1½" dia. wooden wheel, 2½" dia. wooden ball, one each 4½" and 6½" dia. round wooden plaques, black acrylic paint, paintbrushes, wooden bobbin (we used a 14" tall antique bobbin), decorative paper, craft glue, clear matte acrylic spray sealer, four ¾" long flat-head screws, four 18mm black wooden beads, small self-adhesive felt circles, lamp kit without harp, lamp pipe with threaded ends 5" longer than bobbin, hot glue gun, ⅜"w black gimp trim, clip-on lampshade, and beaded fringe.

Allow paint, glue, and sealer to dry after each application.

1. For each lamp, drill ½" dia. holes through center of wheel, ball, and plaques.

2. Paint wheel, ball, and plaques black. If desired, paint bobbin brown, then *Dry Brush*, page 123, with black paint.

3. Cut a circle from paper to fit top of 4½" dia. plaque. Use craft glue to attach paper circle to plaque. Apply sealer to painted items.

4. Spacing evenly, use screws to attach beads to bottom of large plaque for feet. Cover each screw head with a felt circle.

5. For base, twist lock nut from lamp kit onto bottom of lamp pipe. Place large plaque, small plaque, ball, bobbin, then wheel on pipe; glue pieces together to secure. Follow manufacturer's instructions to assemble lamp kit on pipe.

6. Starting at back seam, hot glue gimp around top edge of shade. Hot glue fringe around bottom of shade. Hot glue another length of gimp over top edge of fringe. Place shade on lamp.

DOOR PANEL FRAMES

*B*ecause of their recessed panels and elongated shape, old cabinet doors make natural artwork frames. A border of rustic red paint is applied to the outer molding of the cabinet to create the "frame," while handmade paper provides a pretty background for the inner panel. Cut from wallpaper, rooster motifs are mounted on corrugated cardboard squares.

DECORATIVE CABINET DOOR PANEL

You will need sandpaper, wooden cabinet door (we used a 33" x 15¹/₂" door), tack cloth, miter box and saw, ¹/₂"w decorative molding, spray primer, assorted colors of acrylic paint to coordinate with wallpaper (we used ivory, red, and green), paintbrushes, clear acrylic spray sealer, handmade paper, spray adhesive, craft glue, desired motif wallpaper, corrugated craft cardboard, decorative items to embellish panel (we used feathers), and a sawtooth picture hanger.

Painting instructions indicate the colors we used; substitute paint colors to coordinate with your wallpaper motifs as desired. Allow primer, paint, sealer, and glue to dry after each application.

1. Sand door; wipe with tack cloth.

2. Mitering corners, cut pieces of molding to fit along inner edges of door frame.

3. Apply primer, then two coats of red paint to door frame. Follow *Dry Brush*, page 123, to lightly paint frame with ivory. Paint molding pieces green. Apply sealer to door and molding pieces.

4. Cut a piece from handmade paper to fit in center part of door; use spray adhesive to attach paper to door. Glue molding pieces to door.

5. Centering motifs, cut three equal-size squares from wallpaper; use spray adhesive to attach squares to cardboard. Trim cardboard ³/₄" outside edges of squares. Arrange and glue motifs and decorative items on door.

6. Attach hanger to back of door.

PRINTER'S PASTA TRAY

Showcase your favorite "types" of beans and pastas in an old printer's tray. Simply apply a crackle finish to the wood, fill the compartments with assorted dried foods, and cover with glass. The result will be a "second edition" that's even more newsworthy than the first!

PASTA AND BEAN DISPLAY WINDOW

You will need sandpaper; printer's type drawer; tack cloth; spray primer; yellow, dark yellow, and green acrylic paint; paintbrushes; crackle medium; eyehook and wire picture hanging kit; miter box and saw; wooden dollhouse trim; assorted beans and pastas (we used rainbow rotini, sea shells, elbow macaroni, wagon wheels, spinach fusilli, bow ties, Great Northern beans, black-eyed peas, green and yellow split peas, garbanzo beans, lima beans, kidney beans, small red beans, and pinto beans); glass pieces cut to fit in each large section of tray; and clear silicone sealant.

Allow primer and paint to dry after each application.

1. Sand drawer; wipe with tack cloth.

2. Apply primer to drawer. Using dark yellow for basecoat and yellow for topcoat, follow manufacturer's instructions to crackle drawer.

3. Follow manufacturer's instructions to attach hanger to back of drawer.

4. Cutting to fit and mitering corners, cut pieces of trim to fit along inner edges of each large section of drawer. Paint trim pieces green.

5. Fill compartments with beans and pastas.

6. To attach glass in each large section, apply a thin line of silicone sealant along inner top edges of section; press glass into silicone. Apply a thin layer of silicone to backs of trim pieces. Attach trim over edges of glass. Allow to dry.

PRETTY POTATO MASHER VASE

Corsage vials, colorful glass beads, and a few twists of gold wire are the basic ingredients needed to transform a potato masher into a pretty vase. Perfectly balanced and with a hint of Art Deco styling, this graceful gizmo of Americana deserves to be displayed.

POTATO MASHER VASE

You will need a drill and bits, potato masher with wooden handle, 1¼" dia. glass knob and a screw ½" longer than knob, assorted beads, six 2" long gold eye pins, small needle-nose pliers, 20-gauge gold craft wire, wire cutters, and six plastic corsage vials.

1. Drill a hole in top of masher handle, then use screw to attach knob.

2. For each bead stem, thread 1½" of beads onto eye pin. Use pliers to form a loop in straight end of pin.

3. Cut four 20" lengths of wire. Leaving a 2" tail, twist ends of two lengths of wire together. Repeat for remaining wires. Place first vial between one set of wires 1¾" from top of vial; tightly twist wires together on opposite side of vial. Spacing wires 2" apart, repeat with remaining set of wires. Thread one bead stem onto wires (Fig. 1). Continue to add remaining vials and bead stems.

Fig. 1

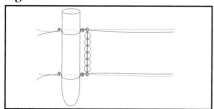

4. Wrap vials around masher, twist wire ends together to secure; trim wire ends.

FANCIFUL MEMO BOARD

*T*he glass in an old picture frame provides an ideal surface for writing notes with a dry-erase marker. Simply decorate the back of the glass as you please and spray it with white paint; then dress up the frame with whimsical stripes and swirls. The result is a fanciful memo board guaranteed to catch the eye of all passersby!

DRY-ERASE BOARD

You will need spray primer, picture frame, assorted colors of acrylic paint, paintbrushes, matte clear acrylic spray sealer, glass to fit in frame, paint pens, and matte-finish white spray paint.

Refer to Painting Techniques, page 123, before beginning project. Allow primer, paint, and sealer to dry after each application. Only use a grease pencil or a dry-erase pen on glass.

1. Apply primer to frame. Paint frame as desired (we painted striped borders, dots, and swirls over our basecoat colors). Apply sealer to frame.

2. Paint design on glass as desired (we used a paint pen to draw swirled lines and the end of a paintbrush handle to paint the dots). Spray painted side of glass white.

3. With unpainted side of glass facing front, mount glass in frame.

Don't overlook flea market items that appear beyond repair. We fashioned this elegant chalkboard from an eyesore picture frame that we refreshed with an easy paint technique. A piece of thin hardboard sprayed with blackboard paint transformed the rescued frame into a handy message center. If you prefer, substitute a corkboard or a mirror.

FRAMED BLACKBOARD

You will need a wooden picture frame, saw, ¼" thick hardboard, spray primer, black spray chalkboard paint, green and black acrylic paint, paintbrushes, soft cloth, metallic gold rub-on finish, clear acrylic spray sealer, and a hot glue gun.

1. Measure height and width of opening on back of frame (Fig. 1). Cut a piece from hardboard the determined measurements.

Fig. 1

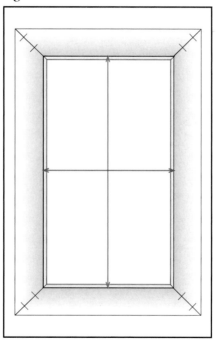

2. Apply primer to smooth side of hardboard piece; allow to dry.

3. Paint primed side of hardboard with chalkboard paint; allow to dry. Apply additional coats of paint as needed for even coverage.

4. Paint frame green; allow to dry.

5. For wash, mix one part black acrylic paint with one part water. Working in small sections and immediately using cloth to wipe section, apply wash to frame for a weathered look; allow to dry.

6. Follow manufacturer's instructions to apply rub-on finish to frame as desired.

7. Apply sealer to frame; allow to dry.

8. Place blackboard in frame; glue along edges on back to secure.

BANISTER POST LAMP

If you want to infuse your home with cottage charm, then crafting this banister post lamp is a step in the right direction. Dress up a dainty shade with handkerchiefs, buttons, and other "de-light-ful" trims to top off a look that glows with homespun style!

BANISTER POST LAMP

You will need sandpaper, 5" square wooden plaque, tack cloth, ivory and light brown acrylic paint, paintbrushes, paste floor wax, 4" square banister piece the desired height for lamp, nails, hammer, drill and bits, bottle-style lamp kit, four assorted handkerchiefs, square lampshade, spray adhesive, ribbon, hot glue gun, assorted buttons, and lace trim.

Allow paint and glue to dry after each application.

1. Sand plaque; wipe with tack cloth. Paint plaque light brown. Apply a thin layer of wax to plaque; paint plaque ivory. Sand plaque on match banister piece.

2. For base, center and nail plaque on bottom of banister.

3. Drill one hole at top center of banister to accommodate stopper from lamp kit. Follow manufacturer's instructions to assemble lamp on banister.

4. Arrange handkerchiefs on shade, trim even with top and sides of shade. Use spray adhesive to attach handkerchief pieces to shade.

5. Tie ribbon into a bow. Glue buttons along edges of handkerchiefs, trim along top and bottom edges of shade, and bow to front top edge of shade. Glue a button to knot of bow.

LAMP-BASE CANDLEHOLDERS

With most lamps, the shade tears or the wiring fails long before the base gives out. Turn those glass or crystal parts into charming, old-timey candleholders. Simply unscrew the pieces and reassemble them in artistic combinations. Top with a votive holder or muffin tin, just right for holding a candle that will give a glow to any setting.

LAMP CANDLEHOLDERS

You will need crystal and milk glass lamps, household cement, metal fluted muffin tins, and clear glass votive holders.

1. Disassemble lamps; remove electrical parts and wiring.

2. Matching and stacking pieces as desired, use household cement to glue lamp pieces, tins, and votive holders together to form candlesticks; allow to dry.

VINTAGE ACCENT PILLOWS

Pretty vintage textiles are staples at flea markets and have loads of decorating potential. With their damaged areas cut away or kept out of sight, tattered treasures such as old-fashioned quilts, chenille bedspreads, and table linens can be made into decorative pillows that you'll love to have around.

VINTAGE LINEN PILLOWS
Square or Rectangular Pillow

You will need vintage linens (we used a quilt top, tablecloth, and embroidered and lace-edged dresser scarves), buttons, and polyester fiberfill.

Use a ¹/₂" seam allowance for all sewing.

1. Cut two desired-size squares or rectangles for pillow front and back from linens (two or more small sections may be seamed together before cutting, if necessary).

2. For pillow flap, choose a linen with a decorative end or corner. Cut flap from end or corner with the cut edge equal to or less than length of top edge of pillow front. Matching raw edges, position flap right side up on right side of pillow front; baste in place. Sew buttons to pillow front as desired.

3. Finish pillow by placing front and back pieces right sides together. Leaving an opening for turning, sew pieces together. Clip corners, turn right side out, and press. Stuff pillow with fiberfill; sew opening closed.

Bolster Pillow

You will need a chenille bedspread, doilies, buttons, and polyester fiberfill.

Use a ¹/₂" seam allowance for all sewing.

1. Cut a 16" x 20" rectangle and two 7" dia. circles from bedspread. Arrange doilies on rectangle and stitch in place; sew buttons to doilies.

2. Matching right sides and leaving an opening in center of seam for turning, sew short edges of rectangle together, forming a tube. Referring to Fig. 1, stitch one circle in each end of tube. Turn pillow right side out, stuff with fiberfill, and sew opening closed.

Fig. 1

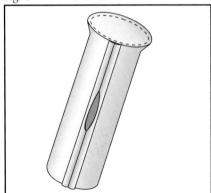

A TASTEFUL TIMEPIECE

*D*o you "knead" a new clock for your kitchen? Turn an old breadboard into a tasteful timepiece! Just glaze, dry, and add self-adhesive numbers. Attach the clock mechanism, and you've got a recipe for timeless appeal.

BREADBOARD CLOCK

You will need sandpaper, round breadboard, tack cloth, white acrylic paint, glazing medium, paintbrushes, drill and bits, clock movement kit with a pendulum, and self-adhesive numbers.

1. Sand board; wipe with tack cloth.

2. For glaze, mix one part white paint with two parts glazing medium; apply glaze to breadboard; allow to dry.

3. Follow manufacturer's instructions to assemble clock on board. Apply numbers to clock.

FRENCH COUNTRY CHANDELIER

*A*s lovely as the light fixtures found in French country rooms, this charming chandelier started out as somebody's throwaway! We freshened it with cream paint and then enriched it with a soft aged finish. Covering the lampshades with handmade paper and slipping a fabric sleeve over the chain enhanced the beauty of this flea market find.

SHADED CHANDELIER

You will need a chandelier with candle sockets and hanging chain, spray primer, ivory spray paint, brown acrylic paint, foam brush, fabric, small self-adhesive lampshades, handmade paper, hot glue gun, and jute twine.

Allow primer and paint to dry after each application.

1. Spray chandelier with primer, then ivory paint. For wash, mix one part water with two parts brown paint; apply to chandelier and wipe immediately with a soft cloth.

2. For chain sleeve, cut a 3"w strip of fabric twice the length of chain to be covered; press ends $1/4$" to wrong side. Matching right sides, use a $1/2$" seam allowance to sew long edges together to form a tube; turn tube right side out. Slide tube onto chain, gathering to fit.

3. Follow manufacturer's instructions to cover lampshades with handmade paper. Glue lengths of jute along top and bottom edges of each shade. Place shades on chandelier.

BEAUTIFUL BUCKET PLANTER

You don't need a green thumb to make a weather-beaten bucket blossom into a pretty planter. Just gather up some paint, a few finials, and an ivy stencil. You'll soon have a charming cachepot guaranteed to make any plant beautiful!

BUCKET PLANTER

You will need sandpaper; metal bucket; tack cloth; brush-on primer; paintbrushes; desired colors of acrylic paint, including green; ivy stencil; stencil brush; drill and bits; three 3" dia. wooden turnings for feet; three 1" long wood screws; and clear acrylic spray sealer.

Refer to Painting Techniques, page 123, before beginning project. Allow primer, paint, and sealer to dry after each application.

1. Sand bucket; wipe with tack cloth.

2. Apply primer to outside of bucket. Paint sections on bucket desired basecoat colors; paint feet.

3. *Stencil* green ivy around center of bucket. Paint stripes and diamond outlines around bucket; use end of paintbrush handle to paint dots for berries among ivy leaves.

4. Drill three evenly spaced holes in bottom of bucket to attach feet. Working from inside, use screws to attach feet to bottom of bucket.

5. Apply two to three coats of sealer to planter.

PLANTER LAMP

*H*ow about cooking up a lamp that will help houseplants thrive in low-light areas? This fanciful planter lamp grew out of an aluminum gelatin-ring mold and cake cover found in a hodgepodge of potential flea market treasures. A timeworn paint finish enhances the lamp's old-fashioned charm.

CAKE COVER AND GELATIN MOLD LAMP

You will need a drill and bits, 10" dia. aluminum cake cover, lamp kit with harp, sandpaper, 9" dia. decorative aluminum gelatin-ring mold, tack cloth, red oxide spray primer, green spray paint, paste floor wax, clear acrylic spray sealer, two lock nuts to fit pipe, two washers slightly larger than hole in mold, 10" long lamp pipe with threaded ends, epoxy putty, lamp finial, and desired plants.

Follow manufacturer's instructions to mix epoxy putty; use putty for all gluing. Allow primer, paint, and sealer to dry after each application.

1. Drill a hole through center of cake cover to accommodate end of lamp harp.

2. Sand cover and mold; wipe with tack cloth. Apply primer to cover and mold, then apply a thin layer of wax. Paint shade and mold green. Lightly sand for an aged look; wipe with tack cloth. Apply sealer to cover and mold.

3. For planter, thread nut, washer, then remaining nut onto one end of pipe. Thread pipe up through hole in center of mold until washer catches on mold; glue in place. Thread remaining washer onto top of pipe and glue to top of mold.

4. Follow manufacturer's instructions to assemble lamp kit on pipe.

5. Place cover on harp and secure with finial.

6. Fill planter with plants.

WASHBOARD WALL CABINET

Put an old washboard back to work as the eye-catching door for this handy cabinet and towel rack! A ready-made shelving unit makes assembly easy, and a dowel creates the towel bar. Refreshed with stain and sealer, this reminder of times past will provide valuable storage — and add interest to your laundry room or kitchen décor.

WASHBOARD CABINET

You will need a wooden washboard, drill and bits, $^3/_4$" dia. dowel, two 1" long wood screws, wood glue, two $^3/_8$" dia. wooden plugs, sandpaper, wooden shelf unit to fit behind washboard (we used a shelf with hanging knobs), wooden knob and a screw $^1/_2$" longer than depth of washboard, tack cloth, stain to match washboard, foam brushes, two 2" long hinges, magnetic door catch, and two picture hangers.

Allow glue and stain to dry after each application.

1. Determine desired height for towel bar on washboard; mark outer side of each leg at determined height. Drill a $^1/_4$" deep, $^3/_8$" dia. hole at center of each mark. Drill a pilot hole through leg at center of each hole.

2. For towel bar, measure between legs of washboard; cut a piece of dowel the determined measurement. Place bar between legs; drive screws into each end of bar through holes. Glue plugs in holes.

3. Lightly sand shelf, towel bar, and knob; wipe with tack cloth. Stain shelf, towel bar, and knob to match washboard.

4. Use hinges to attach washboard to shelf for door. For door handle, drill a hole through edge of door from front to back; use screw to attach knob to door.

5. Aligning pieces, attach flat side of magnetic catch to door and remaining piece to shelf.

6. Attach hangers to top back of cabinet.

43

BASKET SHADE LAMP

Why spend a lot of money on a store-bought lamp when you can make one for much less? A lamp kit at the home improvement store and a bit of imagination are all you need to get started. Fashion a homey illuminant like this from a wooden candlestick and a wicker basket — which are easy to find at flea markets or in your own castaways.

WOODEN CANDLESTICK LAMP

You will need a lamp kit for bottle base, wooden candlestick for lamp base (we used a 4" dia. candlestick), drill and bits, wicker basket for lampshade, lampshade adapter, and a wooden knob for finial.

Use a 40-watt bulb or lower in lamp for safety purposes.

1. Assemble lamp kit in hole for candle on candlestick.

2. Drill a hole at bottom center of basket to accommodate lampshade adapter; use knob to secure adapter to shade.

3. Place shade on lamp.

WINDOW WITH A VIEW

*R*efresh your home with a lovely arrangement of botanical prints. Spray mount the flowery images onto coordinating mat boards, and then place them inside the panes of a weathered window frame. Attach a decorative drawer pull to the wood before hanging, and you're all set to enjoy your new view!

WINDOW-FRAMED PRINTS
You will need a window with panes, mat board, craft knife and cutting mat, spray adhesive, desired prints 1" to 2" smaller than window panes, hot glue gun, drill and bit, decorative drawer pull, and two heavy-duty sawtooth hangers.

1. Clean window frame and both sides of glass; allow to dry.

2. Cut a piece of mat board to fit each pane in window.

3. Use spray adhesive to attach a print to center of each mat.

4. Place matted prints in panes; glue along edges on back to secure.

5. Attach drawer pull to center front and hangers to top back of window.

HANDY STATIONERY CASE

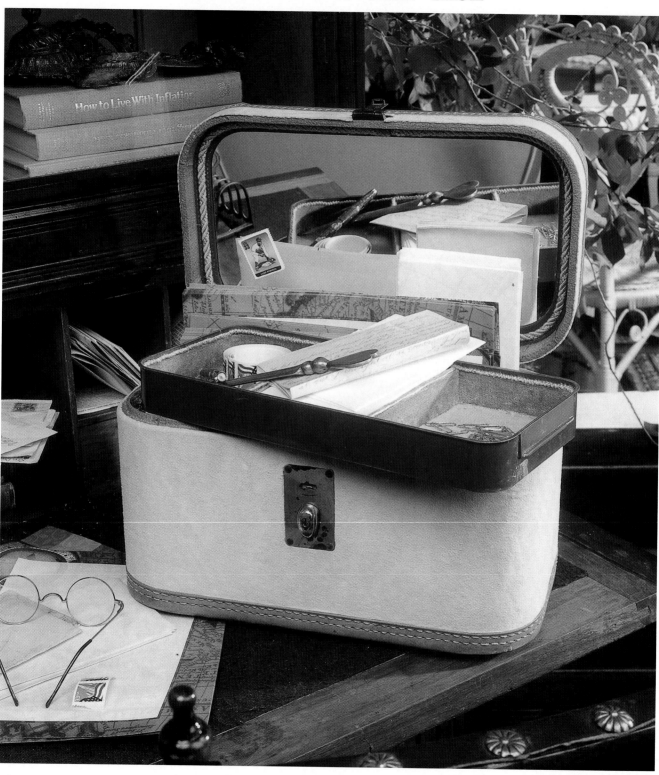

Turn a dated make-up travel case into a handy stationery tote in a few easy steps. Line the inside with upholstery velvet, cover the outside with soft chamois, and attach a jazzy golden tassel. The luxurious look and feel of these materials will encourage you to keep up your letter writing!

STATIONERY TOTE

You will need a vanity case with tray and mirror, velour upholstery fabric, spray adhesive, craft glue, ¹/₂"w gimp trim, decorative cord, chamois hide, and a 6" long tassel.

Refer to Tote Diagrams A and B for all measuring. Use a paintbrush to apply glue.

1. Remove fabric lining from case.

2. Measure length (A) and width (B) of inside bottom of case. Cut a piece from fabric the determined measurements. Apply spray adhesive to wrong side of fabric piece; trimming corners to fit, smooth over inside bottom of case.

3. Measure around inside edge on bottom of case (C), then measure depth of case (D); cut a strip from fabric the determined measurements. Apply spray adhesive to wrong side of strip. Matching one long edge to bottom edge of case, line inside with fabric.

4. Covering raw edges, glue gimp along top edge and cord along bottom edge of fabric. Glue a length of cord along inner edge of lid.

5. Follow Steps 2 and 3 to cover each section of tray. Covering raw edges of fabric, glue lengths of cord along top edge of tray and dividers.

6. To cover outside bottom of case, measure height (E). Measure around case (F) and add ¹/₂". Cut a piece from chamois the determined measurement. Beginning at one back hinge, applying glue to case in small sections, and trimming chamois to fit around hardware, smooth chamois piece around case; trim ends to meet. Repeat to cover top edge of case.

7. Cut a piece of chamois slightly larger than top of case. Measure distance between handles. Cut a slit the determined measurement at center of chamois piece (Fig. 1).

Fig. 1

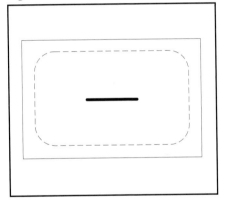

8. Insert handle through slit in chamois. Beginning at seam between handles, applying glue to top in small sections, and trimming chamois to fit around hardware, smooth chamois piece over top of case. Trim edges of chamois even with top.

9. Tie tassel to handle.

TOTE DIAGRAM A

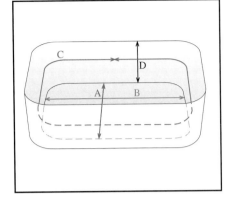

TOTE DIAGRAM B

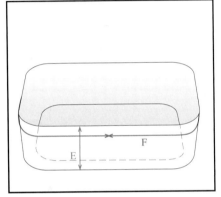

COUNTRY CANDLE TRAY

*I*nvite the warmth of country charm to your living room with our inventive chicken-feeder candle tray. Transform an old farm provision into this delicate decoration by lining the tray with scalloped metal flashing and gluing a fancy wooden emblem to the front. After a light application of wood-tone spray, it's ready for you to fill with sand and arrange your candles!

CHICKEN-FEEDER CANDLEHOLDER
You will need household cement, craft steel, utility scissors, trough-style chicken feeder, tracing paper, decorative wooden cutout, white spray primer, white spray paint, wood-tone spray, clear acrylic spray sealer, and sand.

Allow household cement, paint, wood-tone spray, and sealer to dry after each application.

1. Using household cement to piece as necessary, cut two 1"w strips of craft steel to fit long edges of feeder. Trace the scallop pattern, page 127, onto tracing paper; cut out. Beginning at the center and working outward, use pattern to mark scallops along top edge of steel strips. Use utility scissors to cut along scallops. Use household cement to glue strips along inside edges of feeder.

2. Use household cement to attach cutout to front of feeder. Spray feeder with primer, then white paint. Lightly spray feeder with wood-tone spray, then two coats of sealer.

3. Fill candleholder with 1" of sand; arrange candles in sand.

STYLISH ADDRESS PLAQUE

*F*riends *will never guess that this stylish address plaque was once a useful kitchen tool! Attach a wire hanger to the back of a wooden cheese board, and then embellish the board with gilded house numbers and decorative wooden accents. What a wonderful welcome to your home!*

ADDRESS PLAQUE

You will need two decorative wooden cutouts, wood-tone spray, metallic gold rub-on finish, metal house numbers, wood glue, wooden cheese board, and a picture hanging kit.

1. Spray wooden cutouts with wood-tone spray; allow to dry. Use rub-on finish to add highlights to cutouts and numbers.

2. Use wood glue to attach cutouts to board, then attach numbers.

3. Follow manufacturer's instructions to attach hanging kit to back of address plaque.

FLICKERING LANTERN

For an inventive way to bring the outdoors in, try our charming lantern lamp! Cast a golden glow on your porch or living room through the globe you paint with yellow glass paint. After adding an electric lamp socket and a flickering candelabra lightbulb, you're ready to light the way indoors or out.

LANTERN LAMP

You will need a kerosene camping lantern, yellow glass paint, paintbrush, candelabra socket lamp base, electrical tape, flickering candelabra lightbulb, and a brown lamp replacement cord.

Refer to Lamp Diagram to assemble lamp.

1. Take lantern apart and thoroughly clean all parts to remove any kerosene or oil residue. Reassemble lantern except for globe and top.

2. Paint outside of lantern globe yellow; allow to dry.

3. Wrap one wire on cord around one screw on socket; tighten screw. Repeat to attach remaining wire to opposite side. Wrap socket securely with electrical tape. Screw bulb into socket.

4. With bulb pointing downward, position socket against mantle holders; wrap with tape to secure.

5. Running cord through notch in base of globe holder, replace globe and reattach lantern top.

LAMP DIAGRAM

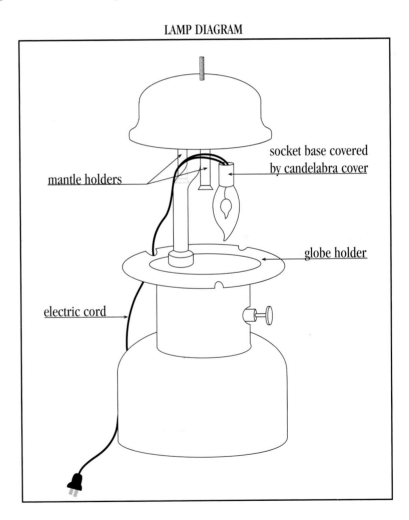

mantle holders

socket base covered by candelabra cover

globe holder

electric cord

COFFEEPOT PLANTERS

*D*on't toss those old coffeepots —
grab some paint and transform them
into stylish planters! Begin with your
favorite colors to create contrasting
bands of paint, then apply a mixture
of glaze and paint and "comb" on
the final designs. Perfect for live
or artificial plants, these vases are
sure to brighten any room.

COFFEEPOT PLANTERS

For each planter, you will need a
coffeepot, spray primer, acrylic paint in
assorted colors (we used yellow, red,
blue, light green, green, and copper),
painter's masking tape, glazing medium,
paintbrushes, foam brush, rubber
combing tool, and clear acrylic
matte spray sealer.

*Allow primer, paint, and sealer to dry
after each application.*

1. Clean pot thoroughly; allow to dry.
Apply primer, then two coats of desired
color of basecoat paint to pot.

2. Apply tape to mask edges of areas
to be combed. For glaze, mix two parts
glazing medium with one part contrasting
paint. Use foam brush to apply glaze to
areas of pot to be combed.

3. Using a smooth motion and even
pressure, pull combing tool through glaze
to form desired pattern; wipe glaze from
comb after each stroke.

4. Remove tape. Use paintbrushes and
glaze to add details to rim, spout, and
base as desired. Apply two coats of
sealer to pot.

LUNCH BOX RECIPE HOLDER

*W*hy keep your favorite recipe cards stashed in a drawer, when they can be at arm's reach in this cheery container? Metal lunch boxes of times past came in interesting shapes, making them fun to decorate today with paint and paper cutouts. A gingham bow adds just the right homespun detail to this charming recipe box!

LUNCH BOX RECIPE HOLDER

You will need household cement, four decorative wooden turnings for feet, metal lunch box, spray primer, black spray paint, green and gold acrylic paint, paintbrushes, decoupage glue, foam brush, desired motifs cut from wrapping paper, clear acrylic spray sealer, and ribbon.

Allow cement, paint, and sealer to dry after each application.

1. Use cement to glue feet to bottom of lunch box.

2. Apply primer, then black paint to box. Paint a green stripe around each foot. Use end of paintbrush handle to paint green dots on feet and box as desired. Paint locks and handle hinges gold.

3. Follow *Decoupage*, page 122, to apply motifs to box.

4. Apply two coats of sealer to box.

5. Tie ribbon into a bow around handle.

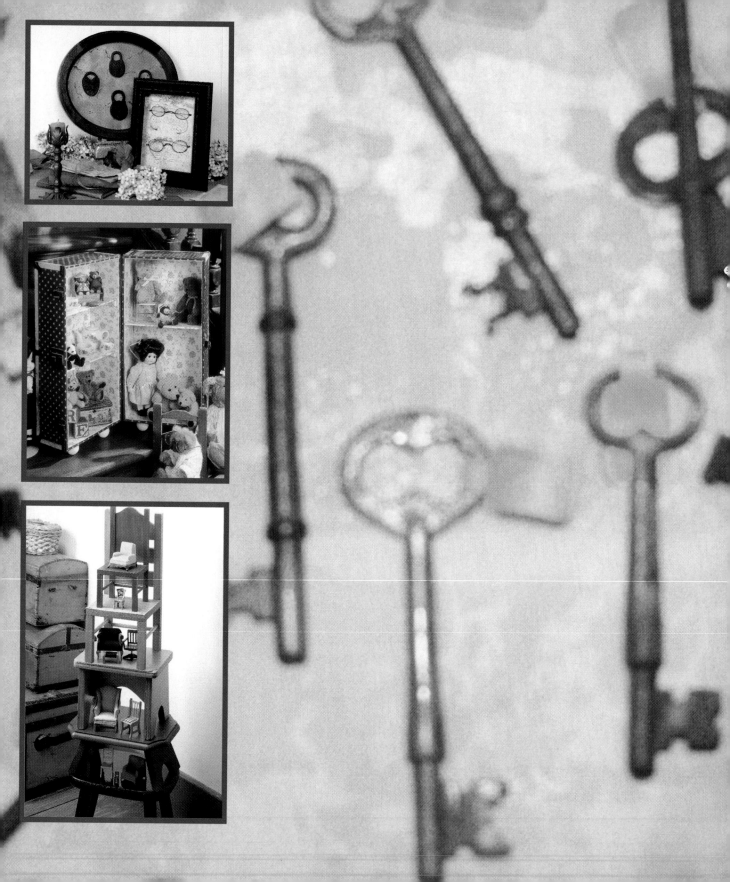

COLLECTIONS

with class

If you're like most flea market fanatics, you have quite a stash of nostalgic keepsakes and unusual knickknacks that you couldn't pass up through the years. Here we reveal the secrets to presenting your collections with class. Using old picture frames, spice racks, and other overlooked has-beens, you can fashion attractive displays that will bring your treasures back into the spotlight!

Looking for a unique way to showcase your child's toys or a set of cherished collectibles? Why not use an old doll trunk to create a darling display case? Simply line the interior of the trunk and shelves with decorative paper, then finish the pleasing presentation by adding painted knob feet.

SHOWCASE TRUNK

You will need spray primer, desired color of acrylic paint, paintbrushes, clear acrylic sealer, eight 1½" dia. wooden ball knobs for feet, metal doll trunk, drill and bits, wood screws, decorative paper, spray adhesive, balsa wood, hot glue gun, and flat wooden molding.

Steps 2 – 5 are for finishing one side of the trunk; repeat steps to finish remaining side. Refer to Trunk Diagram for all measuring.

1. Apply primer, paint, then sealer to feet; allow to dry. Determine which end of trunk will be bottom. Drill four evenly spaced holes through bottom of trunk on each half of trunk. Working from inside, use wood screws to attach feet to trunk.

2. Measure around inside edge on one side of trunk (A), then measure depth of side (B); add ½" to each measurement. Cut a piece from decorative paper the determined measurements. Apply spray adhesive to wrong side of paper piece. Beginning ½" past one corner, matching one long edge to outer edge, and pressing excess paper to back, line inner edges with paper.

3. Measure height (C) and width (D) of inside back; cut a piece from paper the determined measurements. Apply spray adhesive to wrong side of paper piece; smooth over back.

4. Using B and D measurements, cut desired number of shelves from balsa wood. Using spray adhesive to secure paper and overlapping ends at bottom, wrap a piece of decorative paper around each shelf; trim paper even with ends of shelves.

5. Subtract ½" from measurement B. For each shelf, cut two supports from molding the determined measurement. Using spray adhesive to secure paper, wrap supports with decorative paper. Measuring from bottom of trunk, mark support placement guides for each shelf (Fig. 1). Aligning top of support with guide and butting end against back of trunk, glue supports in place. Glue shelves to supports.

Fig. 1

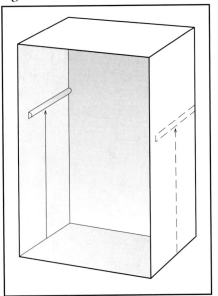

TRUNK DIAGRAM

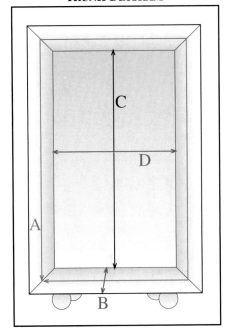

HANKIE PHOTO PILLOW

*S*omething borrowed, something blue ... remember a day that was special to you! Use embroidery floss to cross stitch a wedding photo onto a handkerchief, then sew on a fabric backing and stuff with fiberfill. Dress it up with silk flowers from the ceremony, and you've created a precious memory pillow!

HANDKERCHIEF PILLOW WITH PHOTO

You will need a photograph, square handkerchief, embroidery floss, artificial flower sprigs, buttons, muslin, and polyester fiberfill.

1. Center photograph on right side of handkerchief. Use six strands of floss to work *Cross Stitches*, page 122, along edges of photo to secure. Use floss to attach flower sprigs and buttons around photo.

2. For pillow back, cut a square from muslin $1/2$" larger all around than handkerchief; press edges $1/2$" to wrong side.

3. Place pillow front and pillow back wrong sides together; pin in place. Leaving an opening for stuffing and using a $1/4$" seam allowance, sew pillow front and back together.

4. Referring to Fig. 1 and leaving an opening on same side as first opening, sew pillow 2" from edges to form flange; stuff with fiberfill and sew openings closed.

Fig. 1

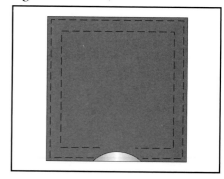

WINDOW OF KEEPSAKES

*P*reserve special memories by using an old window frame to display treasured keepsakes. Apply an aged finish to the wood, and even an assortment of flea market items will bring a sentimental tear to your eye!

WINDOW OF COLLECTIBLES

You will need sandpaper, wooden window frame with glass panes removed, tack cloth, spray primer, ivory and tan acrylic paint, paintbrushes, clear acrylic spray sealer, two heavy-duty picture hangers, and collectibles.

Allow primer, paint, and sealer to dry after each application.

1. Sand frame; wipe with tack cloth.

2. Apply primer, then two coats of tan paint to frame. Follow *Dry Brush*, page 123, to lightly paint frame ivory.

3. Apply two coats of sealer to frame.

4. Attach hangers to back of frame.

5. Hang frame on wall; attach collectibles to wall within frame sections.

STACKED FOR CHARM

You're sure to receive more than a standing ovation when you display your knickknacks on this clever shelf. The tower of footstools in mismatched colors and styles will add a whimsical touch to an entranceway or corner nook.

STACKED STOOLS AND CHAIRS

You will need a small saw, small wooden chairs and stools in varying sizes, and household cement.

1. Cut rungs from fronts of chairs to create display areas.

2. Stack and glue stools, then chairs from largest to smallest; allow to dry.

FRAMED COLLECTIONS

Looking for a new way to showcase pint-sized collectibles? Try mounting them in old wooden frames and exhibiting them in a collector's gallery! Vintage buttons, period postcards, antique keys, and other tiny trinkets are readily accessible at flea markets and make winsome wall or tabletop displays. Create an attractive backdrop for your treasures by covering pieces of cardboard with pretty wallpaper scraps.

FRAMED MINI COLLECTIONS
For each project, you will need corrugated cardboard, scrap of wallpaper, wooden picture frame, spray adhesive, hot glue gun, collectibles, and nylon thread and needle (optional).

1. For background, cut cardboard and wallpaper to fit frame opening; use spray adhesive to attach wallpaper to cardboard.

2. Place background in frame, then glue along edges on back to secure.

3. Arranging collectibles on background as desired; glue or sew in place.

PORTAL TO THE PAST

*O*pen the door to yesterday's memories by equipping a timeworn screen door to display old-fashioned collectibles. To restore the door to its earlier good looks, replace its screen with hardware cloth and apply fresh paint. Use "S" hooks in the sturdy wire mesh to suspend your nostalgic kitchen finds all over the pleasing portal.

SCREEN DOOR FOR COLLECTIBLES

You will need a wooden screen door, hardware cloth, staple gun, 1" long brads, primer, enamel paint, paintbrushes, clear acrylic spray sealer, and "S" hooks.

Allow primer, paint, and sealer to dry after each application.

1. Remove molding and screen from door; discard screen.

2. Cut a piece from hardware cloth to fit door; position on door and staple in place. Use brads to reattach molding pieces.

3. Apply primer, paint, then sealer to door.

4. Use "S" hooks to hang collectibles on door for display.

SPICY KNICKKNACK RACK

This wooden spice rack is just right for displaying a collection of knickknacks, such as antique salt and pepper shakers. The "new do" was easy to create using paint, crackle medium, an ornate wooden accent, and fabric-covered cardboard backing. So start looking at objects in a fresh way. You might be delighted with what you discover!

COLLECTOR'S RACK

You will need sandpaper, wooden spice rack, tack cloth, ivory and green acrylic paint, paintbrushes, crackle medium, decorative wooden cutout, hot glue gun, cardboard, fabric, spray adhesive, and small nails.

1. Sand spice rack; wipe with tack cloth.

2. Using green for basecoat and ivory for topcoat, follow manufacturer's instructions to crackle rack.

3. Paint cutout green, then follow *Dry Brush*, page 123, to paint with ivory paint; glue cutout to rack.

4. For back, cut a piece from cardboard to fit back of rack. Draw around cardboard piece two times on wrong side of fabric; cut out one piece 1" outside drawn lines and remaining piece ¹/₂" inside drawn lines. Apply spray adhesive to wrong side of larger piece; center cardboard on fabric. Cut fabric diagonally across corners; smooth edges to back. Apply spray adhesive to wrong side of remaining fabric piece; smooth over back of covered cardboard piece. Use small nails to secure covered cardboard to back of rack.

STERLING MEMORY SAVER

*P*reserve special memories for years to come in a shadow box created from an old silver casserole holder. Simply place your treasured keepsakes under a piece of clear acrylic sheeting and garnish the nostalgic scene with an attractive ribbon bow. We used a bent spoon to hang our tasteful memento.

SILVER SHADOW BOX FRAME

You will need a footed silver-plated casserole holder, foam core board, craft knife and cutting mat, batting, fabric, hot glue gun, Plexiglas™, mat board, collectibles, 1¼"w wire-edged ribbon, and an artificial flower with leaves.

1. Place holder upside down on foam core board. Draw around inside edge of holder on board; cut out along drawn line.

2. Draw around board on batting and wrong side of fabric; cut out batting along drawn line and fabric 1" outside drawn line.

3. Place fabric piece wrong side up on a flat surface; center batting, then board on fabric. Pulling fabric taut and folding at corners, wrap fabric edges to wrong side of board and glue to secure.

4. Place holder upside down on mat board. Draw around outer edge of holder; cut out along drawn line. Using mat board as a pattern, have a piece of Plexiglas cut to cover front of frame.

5. For back of frame, place holder upside down on mat board piece; glue along inner edges to secure. Turn holder over and press covered board into holder. Arrange and glue collectibles in frame.

6. Glue Plexiglas over front of frame. Tie ribbon into a bow around one leg; glue flower to knot of bow.

NOSTALGIC COMPOSITION

*F*inding little treasures like a frilly lace handkerchief, an age-old photograph, or a pretty string of pearls is part of the fun of browsing flea markets. But what do you do with them when you get them home? Try arranging the odds and ends together in a frame to create a charming storyboard, or use your own keepsakes to preserve a special memory.

NOSTALGIC COLLECTION

You will need corrugated cardboard, wooden picture frame, sheet music, spray adhesive, wood-tone spray, hot glue gun, 1"w ribbon, dried flowers, photo, and collectibles.

1. For background, cut cardboard to fit in frame opening. Overlapping sheets, use spray adhesive to attach sheet music to cardboard; trim edges even with cardboard. Lightly spray background with wood-tone spray and allow to dry.

2. Place background in frame; glue edges on back to secure.

3. Tie ribbon into a bow around flowers.

4. Arrange photo, collectibles, and flowers on background as desired; glue to secure.

TIMEWORN FRAMED PRINTS

*B*efore you pass over those boxes of old frames at the rummage sale, take a look at this great project. Bring new life to abandoned wooden frames with a distressed finish and fabric-covered mats. Cute illustrated prints become the centerpieces for these country additions to your décor.

FRAMED PRINTS

You will need two 11" x 14" wooden picture frames, cream and brown acrylic paint, paintbrushes, sandpaper, tack cloth, two 11" x 14" mats with 8" x 10" openings, fabric, spray adhesive, and two 8" x 10" prints (we used illustrations from a vintage children's book).

Allow paint and sealer to dry after each application.

1. For each frame, lightly paint frame with brown paint. Paint frame cream; sand lightly for a worn look. Wipe frame with tack cloth.

2. Draw around mat and mat opening on wrong side of fabric; cut out 1" outside outer line and 1" inside inner line. Clip inner corners diagonally to line. Apply spray adhesive to wrong side of fabric. Center and smooth fabric onto mat; smooth edges to back of mat.

3. Place mat in frame; mount print in frame.

PEG RACK HANG-UP

*D*on't deny your heart's desire to pick up eye-catching items at the flea market just because you can't imagine what to do with them! Display those pretty potholders, mugs, etc., on an expandable peg rack embellished with stylish fabric accents.

PADDED PEG RACK

You will need an expandable wooden peg rack, hot glue gun, spray primer, two colors of acrylic paint to coordinate with fabric, paintbrushes, clear acrylic spray sealer, cardboard, batting, fabric, ribbon, and collectibles.

Allow primer, paint, and sealer to dry after each application.

1. Expand rack to desired length; glue joints to secure.

2. Apply primer, then two coats of paint to rack. Use remaining color to paint ends of pegs. Apply two coats of sealer to rack.

3. Cut a piece of cardboard to fit each opening in rack. Draw around each cardboard piece on batting and wrong side of fabric. Cut out batting pieces along drawn lines and fabric pieces 2" outside drawn lines.

4. Place one fabric piece wrong side up on flat surface, then center one batting piece and one cardboard piece on fabric. Pulling fabric taut and folding at corners, wrap fabric edges to wrong side of cardboard; glue to secure. Repeat to cover remaining cardboard pieces; glue into openings.

5. Use ribbon to attach collectibles to pegs of rack.

FURNITURE
with imagination

There are two breeds of flea market furniture: diamonds in the rough that simply need to be revived with a new coat of paint or other finishing technique and one-of-a-kind creations cleverly crafted from all kinds of castoffs. The following pages contain lots of innovative ideas to inspire you, but it's ultimately up to you to recognize and develop the potential in the merchandise you see. Rest assured, once you get started, you'll soon be looking at everything in a new light!

SEWING CABINET DESK SET

Foot-powered sewing machines of our grandmothers' day have all but been replaced by electric ones, but their sturdy, functional cabinets can make great desks. Just replace the treadle mechanism with turned wooden legs and add a glass top for smooth writing. For an old-fashioned touch, apply an antique finish to the desk and an old kitchen chair. Pad the seat for extra comfort.

DESK AND CHAIR SET
Sewing Machine Desk

You will need a treadle sewing machine cabinet, sandpaper, tack cloth, four leg mounting brackets, four wooden screw-in legs, spray primer, white and green acrylic paint, paintbrushes, glazing medium, natural sponge pieces, clear acrylic spray sealer, decorative drawer pulls, handmade paper, and a piece of tempered glass to fit top of desk.

Allow primer, paint, and sealer to dry after each application.

1. Remove metal stand from bottom of cabinet; discard. Sand cabinet; wipe with tack cloth.

2. Use brackets to attach legs to cabinet.

3. Apply primer, then white paint to desk. For glaze, mix one part glazing medium with one part green paint. Dampen sponge with glaze, squeeze out excess, then wipe cabinet with sponge.

4. Apply two coats of sealer to cabinet.

5. Replace drawer pulls.

6. Tear a piece from paper to fit top of desk. Place paper, then glass on desk.

Padded Chair

You will need sandpaper, wooden chair, tack cloth, spray primer, white and green acrylic paint, paintbrushes, glazing medium, natural sponge pieces, clear acrylic spray sealer, kraft paper, batting, fabric, and a staple gun.

Allow primer, paint, and sealer to dry after each application.

1. Sand chair; wipe with tack cloth.

2. Apply primer, then white paint to chair. For glaze, mix one part glazing medium with one part green paint. Dampen sponge with glaze, squeeze out excess, then wipe chair with sponge.

3. Apply two coats of sealer to chair.

4. For seat cover pattern, draw around seat on kraft paper. Using pattern, cut several pieces from batting and one piece from fabric 3" outside edges of pattern.

5. Place batting on seat; center fabric over seat. Folding fabric to fit around legs and stapling fabric edges to bottom of seat, cover seat with fabric.

PLENTIFUL POCKETS ROOM DIVIDER

Turn an old door into an attractive room divider covered with handy pockets. Just add shelves at the base to make it freestanding and replace the screen with a fabric panel mounted with tension rods.

POCKET ROOM DIVIDER

You will need a wooden screen door, $1^1/2$" long wood screws, two wooden shelves the same width as door for base with apron between brackets, sandpaper, tack cloth, spray primer, cream spray paint, white acrylic paint, paintbrushes, crackle medium, 4 yds. of fabric for panel, 2 yds. of fabric for pockets, buttons, and two spring tension rods.

Allow primer and paint to dry after each application. Use a $^1/4$" seam allowance for all sewing.

1. Remove screen and hardware from door.

2. For frame, use screws to attach upside-down shelves to door through apron.

3. Sand frame; wipe with tack cloth. Apply primer to frame. Using cream spray paint for basecoat and white acrylic paint for topcoat, follow manufacturer's instructions to crackle frame.

4. For panel, measure width of opening; add 1". Measure height of opening; multiply by 2. Cut a piece from fabric the determined measurements. Press long edges $^1/4$" to wrong side; press $^1/4$" to wrong side again and topstitch in place. Matching right sides, sew short edges together; turn right side out. With seam at bottom, press panel flat.

5. For each pocket, cut a 10" x $14^1/2$" piece from fabric. For flap, press one short edge $^1/4$" to wrong side, then

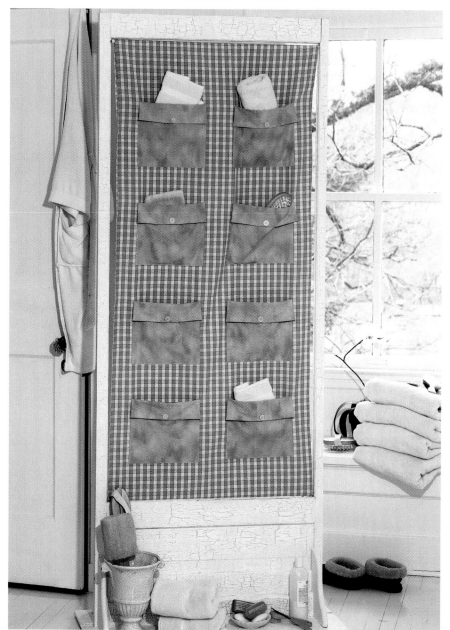

press 3" to right side. Sew along side edges of flap; clip corners and turn right side out. Topstitch hemmed edge of flap in place. Press bottom and raw edges of sides $^1/4$" to wrong side; press flap $2^1/2$" to right side.

6. Arrange and pin pockets on one side of panel. Being careful to not catch flaps, topstitch along side and bottom edges of each pocket; sew buttons to flaps.

7. Use rods to hang panel in opening of frame.

HANDY HAMPER TABLE

Give a humble woven laundry hamper a new purpose in life! To turn it into a classy table for the boudoir or bath, add wooden feet, a pretty painted finish, a silken tassel, and a glass top.

HAMPER TABLE

You will need a large woven clothes hamper with wooden lid, ¼" plywood, saw, wood glue, drill and bits, four 3" dia. wooden turnings for feet, four washers with ¼" dia. hole, 1½" long wood screws, white spray primer, desired color of acrylic paint for hamper, paintbrushes, glazing medium, brown acrylic paint, combing tool, clear acrylic spray sealer, 4½" long tassel, clear self-adhesive surface protectors, and tempered glass for tabletop.

Allow glue, primer, paint, glaze, and sealer to dry after each application.

1. Remove handles from hamper.

2. Draw around bottom of hamper on plywood; cut out ¼" inside drawn lines. Glue wood piece to bottom of hamper. Drill four evenly spaced holes in bottom of hamper to attach feet. Working from inside and placing a washer on each screw, use screws to attach feet to bottom of hamper.

3. Apply primer, then two coats of paint to hamper.

4. For glaze, mix one part glazing medium with one part brown paint. Apply glaze to one foot. Using a smooth motion and even pressure, pull combing tool through glaze to form desired pattern; wipe glaze from comb after each stroke. Repeat to paint remaining feet and create desired design on top of hamper.

5. Apply two coats of sealer to hamper.

6. Glue hanger of tassel to underside of lid at center of opening edge.

7. Adhere surface protectors to lid; place glass on hamper.

SWEET DREAMS

Swinging café doors were once a fixture of American homes, loved for their convenience and graceful lines. Now, they can be retrieved from the basement or attic and converted into a lovely headboard. Painted a soft sage green and graced with a heart-shaped wreath of flowers, this bit of nostalgia is sure to make your dreams sweet.

CAFÉ DOOR HEADBOARD

You will need wood glue, two 3" dia. wooden rings, two 3" dia. wooden flowerpots, two 3" dia. wooden finials, two 5' long $2\frac{1}{2}$" square wooden posts, set of café-style doors (each of our doors is $38\frac{1}{4}$"h x $17\frac{3}{4}$"w), saw, 1" x 2" lumber, $1\frac{1}{2}$" long and $3\frac{1}{2}$" long wood screws, two 6' long pipe clamps, drill and bits, white spray primer, ivory and green acrylic paint, paintbrushes, clear spray matte sealer, and a heart-shaped wreath.

Allow glue, primer, paint, and sealer to dry after each application.

1. Glue one ring, one flowerpot, then one finial to top of each post.

2. Remove hardware from doors. Place doors together, wrong side up, on a flat surface. Measure height at center of doors; subtract 1". Cut a piece from 1" x 2" lumber the determined measurement. Use $1\frac{1}{2}$" long screws to attach lumber to doors along center edges (Fig. 1).

Fig. 1

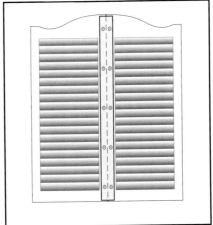

3. Referring to Fig. 2, place 1" x 2" lumber under doors for spacers. Aligning posts, place posts along edges of doors. Use pipe clamps to hold posts against doors. Spacing evenly, drill five pilot holes from outside of posts into outside edges of doors; use $3\frac{1}{2}$" long screws to secure in place, countersinking screws into posts. Remove clamps.

Fig. 2

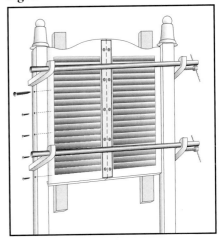

4. Apply primer to headboard. Paint headboard green, then follow *Dry Brush*, page 123, to paint headboard ivory. Apply two coats of sealer to headboard.

5. Hang wreath on headboard.

BEDTIME QUILT RACK

*D*oes your passion for quilts have you searching for innovative ways to show them off? Let them rest on an eye-catching rack fashioned from a twin headboard and footboard set. A dowel rod added in the middle provides additional hanging space.

BED FRAME QUILT RACK
You will need a miter box and saw, 1" x 4" lumber, drill and wood bits, screws, twin-size wooden headboard and footboard, 1" dia. dowel, wood glue, wood putty, sandpaper, tack cloth, white primer, ivory acrylic paint, and a paintbrush.

To determine length of wood screws needed, measure thickness of wood pieces to be joined and subtract ¹/₄". Drill pilot holes before inserting screws into wood. Allow glue, wood putty, primer, and paint to dry after each application.

1. For side pieces of quilt rack, cut two 7½" and two 14⅜" pieces from lumber. Mark center of 14⅜" pieces, then cut ends of each piece at a 45° angle (Fig. 1); use wood bit to drill a hole through pieces at each center mark.

Fig. 1

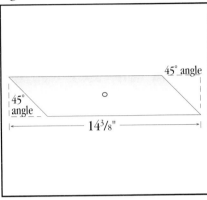

2. Refer to Fig. 2 and use screws to attach side pieces between headboard and footboard, countersinking screws into posts.

Fig. 2

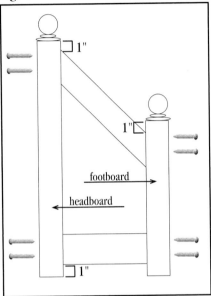

3. For hanging rod, measure across rack from outer edge to outer edge of top side pieces (Fig. 3); cut a length of dowel the determined measurement. Insert dowel through holes; glue to secure.

Fig. 3

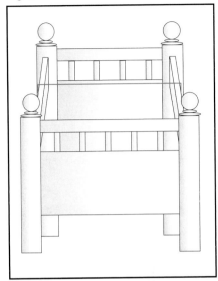

4. Use wood putty to fill in holes and to cover screw heads. Lightly sand rack; wipe with tack cloth. Apply primer, then two coats of ivory paint to rack. Lightly sand rack for a worn look; wipe with tack cloth.

PATCHWORK SLIPCOVER

Is that Parson's chair just a bit too plain? Dress it up with a slipcover made from a patchwork quilt. Whether your stitchery was handed down through the family or found at the flea market, it'll blossom in its useful new role. This appealing accent is sure to become the favorite seat in the house.

PARSON'S CHAIR SLIPCOVER

You will need a chair, kraft paper, fabric to coordinate with quilt, "cutter" quilt (damaged or worn quilt from which intact areas may be salvaged).

Instructions are for covering a Parson's chair with a straight back.

Refer to Chair Diagram for all measuring. Make all patterns from kraft paper; label each pattern piece. Use a $1/2$" seam allowance for all sewing unless otherwise indicated.

1. Measure chair seat at front (A) and back (B), then measure depth of seat (C); add 1" to each measurement. Use measurements to make seat pattern.

2. Measure from back of chair seat, over back of chair and down to floor (D); add $1/2$". Measure across back of seat (B). Use measurements to make chair back cover pattern.

3. Measure along side of chair seat (F); add 5". Measure from top of chair seat to floor (E); add $1/2$". Use measurements to make side skirt pattern.

4. Add 1" to measurement A and $1/2$" to measurement E. Use measurements to make front skirt pattern.

5. For underskirt, multiply measurement F by 2; add measurement A and 1". Add 1" to measurement E. Using measurements, cut underskirt piece from fabric. Press one long edge $1/4$" to wrong side; press $1/4$" to wrong side again and stitch in place. Repeat for short edges. Use seat pattern to cut seat piece from fabric. Matching right sides and raw edges, sew underskirt to front and side edges of seat piece.

6. Measure around chair back at widest point; divide by 2, then add 1". Measure from chair seat to top of chair; multiply by 2, then add 1". Cut a piece of fabric the determined measurements. Matching right sides and short edges, fold fabric in half. Sew along sides to form back cover. Referring to Fig. 1, press each corner flat. Stitch across point to form box corner; trim $1/4$" from stitching line. Turn cover right side out.

Fig. 1

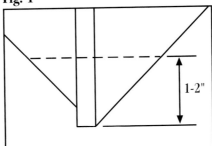

7. Matching right sides and raw edges, center seat on one side of cover; sew pieces together. Press remaining edge of cover $1/4$" to wrong side; press $1/4$" to wrong side again and stitch in place. Place fabric slipcover on chair.

8. Positioning patterns to best utilize quilt design, cut two pieces (one in reverse) using side skirt pattern and one piece each using remaining patterns.

9. Follow *Binding*, page 124, to bind bottom, then side edges of back and skirt pieces.

10. Centering back on back edge of seat piece and matching right sides and raw edges, sew back to seat. Aligning front edge of skirt sides to front edge of seat and matching right sides and raw edges, sew sides to seat. Centering front skirt on front edge of seat and matching right sides and raw edges, sew skirt to seat. Fold raw edges of skirt extensions $1/2$" to wrong side; stitch in place. Place quilt slipcover on chair.

11. For ties, cut six 2" x 24" strips from fabric. For each tie, match wrong sides and long edges and press strip in half; unfold. Matching wrong sides, press long edges to center fold. Press ends $1/4$" to wrong side; refold strip and topstitch edges together.

12. Stitch one tie to top corner on wrong side of each skirt extension; tie into a bow at back of chair.

13. Stitch one pair of ties to each side of chair back cover; tie into bows.

CHAIR DIAGRAM

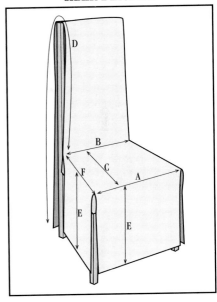

Lend a hint of romance to an old wrought-iron chair by adding a dreamy, ruffled seat cushion. A fresh coat of spray paint, in a color that coordinates with your fabric, gives new life to forgotten patio furniture.

WROUGHT-IRON CHAIR AND CUSHION

You will need sandpaper, wrought-iron chair without arms, tack cloth, spray primer, desired color of spray paint for basecoat and desired color of acrylic paint for details, paintbrushes, clear acrylic spray sealer, kraft paper, 1" thick foam, fabric, and $\frac{1}{4}$" dia. cord.

Allow primer, paint, and sealer to dry after each application.

1. Sand chair to remove any rust; wipe with tack cloth.

2. Apply primer, then two coats of spray paint to chair. Use acrylic paint to add details or paint sections of chair as desired. Apply sealer to chair.

3. For cushion pattern, draw around chair seat on kraft paper. Use pattern to cut cushion from foam. Draw around pattern twice on wrong side of fabric; cut out $\frac{3}{4}$" outside drawn lines for top and bottom cushion pieces.

4. For welting, measure around all edges of cushion; add 4". Piecing as necessary, cut a $2\frac{1}{2}$"w bias strip from fabric, and a length of cord the determined measurement. Press one end of strip $\frac{1}{2}$" to the wrong side. Beginning $\frac{1}{2}$" from pressed end, center cord on wrong side of strip. Fold strip over cord. Beginning $\frac{1}{2}$" from pressed end, use a zipper foot to baste close to cord along length of strip. Trim seam allowance to $\frac{1}{4}$".

5. Beginning with pressed end of welting and matching raw edges, pin welting to right side of top cushion piece (Fig. 1). Trimming to fit, insert unfinished end of welting into folded end of welting (Fig. 2). Baste welting in place close to cord.

Fig. 1

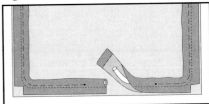

Fig. 2

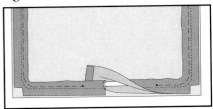

6. For ruffle, measure around sides and front of cushion, then multiply by 2.5; cut a 6"w strip the determined measurement. Press ends and one long edge of strip $\frac{1}{4}$" to the wrong side two times, then stitch in place. To gather ruffle, baste $\frac{1}{4}$" and $\frac{3}{8}$" from raw edge. Pull basting threads, gathering ruffle to fit sides and front of cushion.

7. Matching right sides and raw edges, baste ruffle to top cushion piece. Placing cushion pieces together and leaving open along back, sew pieces together. Clip corners, turn right side out, insert foam, and sew opening closed.

PATIO SET PIZZAZZ

That drab table and chair that went unnoticed before are sure to get a second glance after being revived with paint and decoupaged gift-wrap posies. Hand-painted stripes give both pieces pizzazz, so they won't be wallflowers anymore!

BISTRO CHAIR AND TABLE

You will need spray primer, two colors of acrylic paint to coordinate with wrapping paper, paintbrushes, wooden folding chair with slatted back and bottom, small round wooden table, natural sponge pieces, wrapping paper, decoupage glue, foam brushes, and clear acrylic spray sealer.

Allow primer, paint, glue, and sealer to dry after each application.

Chair

1. Apply primer, then two coats of paint to chair. Paint stripes on chair back as desired.

2. Cut a strip from paper to cover each chair slat. Follow *Decoupage*, page 122, to apply strips to slats.

3. Apply two coats of sealer to chair.

Table

1. Apply primer to table. Paint table desired color. *Sponge Paint*, page 124, outer 2$^1/_2$" of tabletop with coordinating color of paint; paint stripes along edge of tabletop.

2. Draw around tabletop on wrong side of paper; cut out 2" inside drawn line. Follow *Decoupage*, page 122, to apply paper piece to tabletop. *Decoupage* a piece of paper around spindle.

3. Apply two coats of sealer to table.

KITCHEN TOWEL TREE

*K*eep dish towels at your fingertips with a handy kitchen tree made from an old banister post. Apply a distressed finish to the pole before attaching the clever hooks, which are actually "leftover" forks.

KITCHEN TOWEL RACK

You will need 1" long wood screws, decorative wooden plaque for top, 1" thick oval plaque for base, wooden banister post, sandpaper, tack cloth, primer, cream and grey acrylic paint, paintbrushes, paste floor wax, clear acrylic sealer, pliers, silver-plated dinner forks, upholstery tacks, and a hammer.

Allow paint to dry after each application.

1. Use wood screws to attach plaques to ends of post.

2. Sand rack; wipe with tack cloth. Apply primer, then two coats of grey paint to rack.

3. Apply a thin coat of wax to rack, then paint with cream paint. Lightly sand for a weathered look; wipe with tack cloth. Apply two coats of sealer to rack.

4. For each towel hook, use pliers to bend outer tines of one fork into an outward curve. Bend handle of fork to form hook. Use upholstery tacks to attach hook to rack.

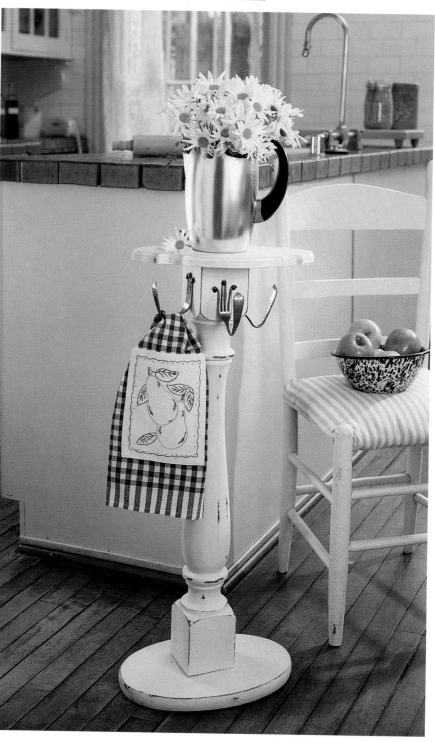

NOSTALGIC ICEBOX

Before there were electric refrigerators, having a wooden icebox was a luxury. Now, you can transform one of these old coolers into a functional and decorative furniture accent! Easy color wash and sanding techniques give the conversation piece its timeworn look.

DISTRESSED ICEBOX

You will need sandpaper, wooden icebox, tack cloth, ivory and brown acrylic paint, paintbrushes, paste floor wax, and clear acrylic spray sealer.

Allow paint and sealer to dry after each application.

1. Sand icebox; wipe with tack cloth.

2. Paint box brown. Apply a thin layer of wax to box; paint box ivory.

3. Lightly sand box for a worn look.

4. Apply two coats of sealer to icebox.

CATCHALL CABINET BENCH

Remodeling your kitchen? Don't toss out that old, outdated cabinet. Turned on its back, the sturdy unit makes a handy storage bench for your mud room or entryway. Just coat the cabinet with primer, sponge on a mixture of paint and glaze, and construct a padded seat using foam, fabric, and plywood. Drill some 2" openings in the kickplate, and you have a nifty umbrella stand as well as a catchall storage bench.

MUD ROOM BENCH

You will need a wooden kitchen base cabinet with door, $1/4$" plywood, saw, wood glue, 1" long finishing nails, drill with 2" dia. hole saw, 1"w wooden corner molding, wood putty, sandpaper, tack cloth, spray primer, green acrylic paint, glazing medium, natural sponge pieces, 4" foam for cushion, fabric, staple gun, $3/4$" long wood screws, 12" of 1"w grosgrain ribbon, and a 1" dia. washer.

Allow glue, wood putty, primer, and sealer to dry after each application.

1. Draw around top, bottom, and back of cabinet on plywood; cut out pieces along drawn lines. Glue, then nail pieces to cabinet. Measure length and width of door; subtract 1" from each measurement, then cut a piece from plywood the determined measurements.

2. Place cabinet on its back. Use hole saw to cut three holes in kick plate of cabinet for umbrella holders.

3. *Hinges of door will determine back of bench. Refer to Bench Diagram to attach molding pieces to bench.* Trimming to fit, glue lengths of molding along sides, then bottom edges on front of bench. Notching ends at top and bottom corners, glue lengths of trim to top and bottom side edges. Nail all trim pieces in place to secure.

4. Apply wood putty over heads of nails. Sand bench; wipe with tack cloth. Apply primer to bench.

5. For glaze, mix one part green paint with two parts glazing medium. Use dampened sponge to rub glaze on cabinet; wring sponge out, then pounce sponge over wet glaze to make texture on cabinet; allow to dry.

6. For cushion, draw around remaining plywood piece on foam and wrong side of fabric; cut out foam along drawn line and fabric 6" outside drawn line.

7. Place fabric, wrong side up, on a flat surface. Center foam, then plywood on fabric. Pulling taut, fold edges, then corners of fabric to back of plywood and staple in place. Working from back of door, use screws to attach cushion to front of door.

8. For handle, cross ribbon ends to form a loop; glue ends at center front on wrong side of opening edge of door. Place washer on a screw; drive screw into door through ribbon ends.

BENCH DIAGRAM

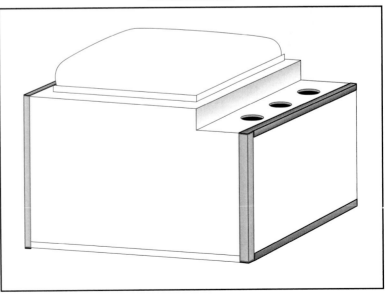

UPDATED OTTOMAN

Kick up your feet and relax awhile on this comfy, stylish ottoman! An outdated round footstool is easy to find at a flea market or garage sale, and it's even easier to make into a fashionable and functional furnishing. Simply pad the top with batting and cover with coordinating fabrics. Gathers and buttons add sophisticated details to the sides.

COVERED OTTOMAN

You will need a round ottoman, batting, two coordinating fabrics, string, fabric marking pencil, needle and heavy-duty thread, $1/4$" dia. cording, $1\frac{1}{4}$" dia. fabric-covered button kit for four buttons, $1\frac{1}{2}$" dia. fabric-covered button kit for one button, and a staple gun.

Use a $1/2$" seam allowance for all sewing.

1. Measure height of ottoman, then measure around ottoman; cut a piece from batting the determined measurements. Cut a piece from one fabric 3" wider and 1" longer than batting piece.

2. Measure across center of ottoman; add 1". Cut a square from batting and coordinating fabric the determined measurement. Divide measurement by 2, then use measurement and follow *Cutting a Fabric Circle*, page 122, to cut one circle each from batting and fabric squares.

3. Wrap batting piece around ottoman; stitch ends together. Position batting circle on ottoman; stitch edge of circle to batting piece.

4. Matching right sides, sew short edges of fabric piece together to form sleeve; press seam open and turn right side out.

5. Cut four pieces of fabric 4" wide and 3" longer than height of ottoman. Matching right sides, sew long edges together to form tube; turn right side out. Centering seam at back, press each tube. Covering seam on sleeve, evenly space tubes around sleeve; baste in place at top and bottom of each tube.

6. For welting, cut a length of cording and a 2"w bias fabric strip (pieced as necessary) 4" longer than ottoman circumference.

7. Press one end of fabric strip $1/2$" to wrong side. Beginning $1/2$" from pressed end, center cording on wrong side of strip. Fold strip over cording; use a zipper foot to baste close to cording. Trim seam allowance to $1/2$".

8. Beginning with unpressed end and matching raw edges, pin welting to right side of fabric circle (Fig. 1).

Fig. 1

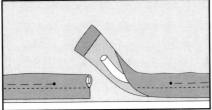

9. Trimming to fit, insert unfinished end of welting into folded end (Fig. 2). Baste welting in place close to cording.

Fig. 2

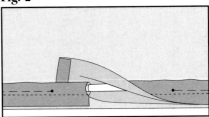

10. Matching right sides, pin edge of circle to top edge of sleeve; sew edges together. Turn right side out and press.

11. Follow manufacturer's instructions to cover buttons with fabric. Sew large button at center top of ottoman cover.

12. Place cover over ottoman. Pulling fabric taut, smooth edges to bottom of ottoman and staple in place. Gathering tube and wrapping thread around gathers to secure, sew one button at center of each tube.

FASHIONABLE FIREPLACE SCREEN

Looking for something to spruce up the fireplace? Try making a decorative screen from an old air-intake panel and a pair of wooden shelf brackets. Tree-shaped turnings make novel finials for the piece, which is finished with a simple glazing technique.

FIREPLACE SCREEN

You will need sandpaper, wooden air-intake panel, tack cloth, 1" x 2" lumber, 1" long screws, spray primer, two 12" wooden shelf brackets, two 3" tall wooden tree-shaped turnings, green spray paint, glazing medium, green acrylic paint, paintbrushes, waxed paper, drill and ³⁄₈" dia. bit, wood glue, two 1" long x ³⁄₈" dia. wooden dowel pieces, six ³⁄₄" x 4" brass hinges, and clear acrylic spray sealer.

Allow primer, paint, and sealer to dry after each application.

1. Sand panel; wipe with tack cloth. Cut two pieces of 1" x 2" lumber to fit side edges of panel. Working from back, use screws to attach pieces to back of panel.

2. Apply primer to panel, brackets, and turnings; spray paint pieces green.

3. For glaze, mix one part glazing medium with one part green acrylic paint. Working in small sections and immediately dabbing section with a piece of crumpled wax paper, apply glaze to frame of panel and remaining painted pieces; allow to dry.

4. Drill one hole at center bottom of each turning and center top on each side of panel. Glue dowels in holes in panel, then glue turnings on dowels.

5. Use hinges to attach brackets to sides of panel.

6. Apply sealer to screen.

FLORAL MAGAZINE STAND

This magazine stand was covered with dust and cobwebs when we found it at a secondhand store, but a little paint and decoupage was all it took to give it today's popular cottage look.

MAGAZINE STAND

You will need ivory, green, pink, and gold acrylic paint; paintbrushes; wooden magazine stand; gold paint pen; color photocopy of camellia print (page 126) enlarged or reduced to desired size; decoupage glue; foam brush; fruitwood gel stain; and clear matte acrylic spray sealer.

Refer to Painting Techniques, page 123, before beginning project. Allow paint and sealer to dry after each application.

1. Paint stand green. Use ivory and pink paint and gold paint pen to accent sides and turnings on stand.

2. Cut motif from photocopy. Follow *Decoupage*, page 122, to attach motif to stand.

3. Use gold paint to add details to stand. Follow manufacturer's instructions to apply a light coat of stain to stand. Apply two coats of sealer to stand.

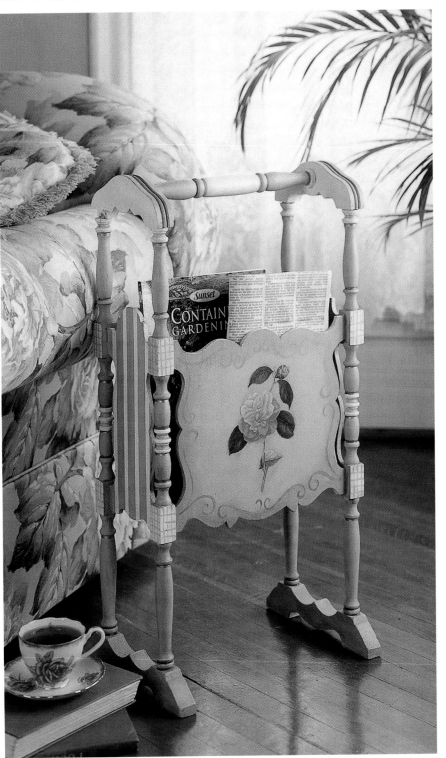

DRAWER OTTOMAN

Once a spacious dresser drawer, this unique footrest now holds thick foam padding wrapped with linen toile. Create a timeworn finish using our easy painting technique, and then add a set of turned wooden legs to heighten the classic look.

DRAWER OTTOMAN

You will need a wooden drawer, leg mounting brackets, four 6$^{1}/_{8}$"h wooden screw-in legs, sandpaper, tack cloth, tan and brown acrylic paint, paintbrushes, paste floor wax, wood-tone spray, clear acrylic spray sealer, eight 2" long "L" brackets, $^{3}/_{8}$" plywood, 4" thick foam, fabric, and a staple gun.

Allow paint, wood-tone spray, and sealer to dry after each application.

1. Remove handles from drawer. For base, use brackets to attach legs to bottom corners of drawer.

2. Sand base; wipe with tack cloth. Paint base brown, apply a thin layer of wax to base, then paint base tan. Sand base for a weathered look; wipe with tack cloth.

3. Spray base with wood-tone spray, then sealer.

4. Matching edges of brackets with top edge of base, attach two "L" brackets to each inside edge of base (Fig. 1). Replace handles on base.

Fig. 1

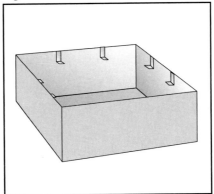

5. Measure length and width of inside base (Fig. 2). Cut a piece from plywood and foam the determined measurements.

Fig. 2

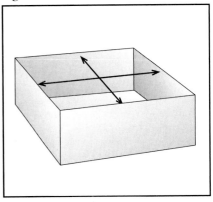

6. Draw around plywood on wrong side of fabric. Cut out 6" outside drawn lines. Place fabric, wrong side up, on a flat surface. Center foam, then plywood on fabric. Fold edges, then corners of fabric to back of plywood and staple in place. Place cushion in base.

NOTEWORTHY PIANO BENCH

To add character to a music lover's favorite spot in your home, resurrect an old piano bench! Just apply paint to the apron and legs and cover the lid with wallpaper. Apply sheet music over the wallpaper for a "noteworthy" finishing touch.

PIANO MUSIC BENCH

You will need sandpaper, piano bench, tack cloth, primer, cream and black acrylic paint, paintbrushes, wood-tone spray, pre-pasted wallpaper, decoupage glue, sheet music and music cover, and a foam brush.

Allow primer, paint, wood-tone spray, and decoupage glue to dry after each application.

1. Sand piano bench and wipe with tack cloth; apply primer. Paint apron, legs, and supports cream. Paint bands of black paint around legs, if desired. Apply wood-tone spray to painted areas.

2. Cut wallpaper 3" larger on all sides than piano bench lid. Wrapping edges to underside, follow manufacturer's instructions to apply wallpaper to lid.

3. Follow *Decoupage*, page 122, to apply sheet music and cover to lid, then sheet music to supports and upper portion of legs.

COTTAGE FOOTSTOOL

You can create a charming cottage footstool simply by recycling an old wooden planter. Begin by turning the timeworn container over and applying paint and fabric accents on each side. Top the stool with a fabric-covered foam pad, and you'll have a footrest to enjoy for years to come!

PLANTER FOOTSTOOL

You will need sandpaper, square wooden planter with molding-trimmed panels, tack cloth, spray primer, one light and one dark color of acrylic paint to coordinate with fabric, paintbrushes, clear acrylic spray sealer, fabric, spray adhesive, fabric glue, $1/8$"w braid to coordinate with fabric, 4" thick foam, staple gun, and $1/2$" dia. cord to coordinate with fabric.

Allow primer, paint, sealer, and glue to dry after each application. Bottom of planter will be top of stool.

1. Sand planter; wipe with tack cloth.

2. For stool base, apply primer, then two coats of light paint to planter. Paint panel trim with dark paint.

3. Apply two coats of sealer to base.

4. For each side of planter, cut a piece from fabric to fit in panel. Apply spray adhesive to wrong side of fabric piece; center and smooth onto planter. Glue braid along raw edges of fabric.

5. For cushion, draw around top of base on foam and wrong side of fabric. Cut out foam 1" outside drawn line and fabric 5" outside drawn line.

6. Place foam on base; center fabric over foam. Pulling fabric taut and gathering corners, staple fabric edges along top edge of base; trim fabric edges as necessary. Glue cord over raw edges of fabric, covering staples.

STYLISH SHUTTER CABINET

Who said louvered shutters were just for windows! Created using a quartet salvaged from a resale shop, this stylish hutch offers both attractiveness and practicality. The easy do-it-yourself project is ideal for storing your glassware.

SHUTTER CABINET

You will need four window shutters
(we used 12" x 39" shutters), $^1/_2$" plywood,
$^1/_2$"w flat molding, 1" long brads, drill and
bits, wood glue, $1^1/_4$" long wood screws,
$^1/_4$" hardboard, eight 1" long "L" brackets,
four utility hinges, two decorative wooden
shelf brackets, primer, white acrylic paint,
paintbrushes, and two cabinet
door handles.

*Drill a $^1/_8$" pilot hole and fill with wood
glue before inserting each screw. Allow
glue, primer, and paint to dry after each
application.*

1. Measure shutter width. For top and
bottom of cabinet, cut two pieces of
plywood the same width as shutter and
twice as long (for example, if shutter is
12" wide, cut plywood 12" x 24").

2. Cut two shelves from plywood
$^1/_2$" narrower than top and bottom (for
example, if top and bottom are 12" x 24",
shelves should be $11^1/_2$" x 24"). Cut a
length of molding to fit one long edge of
each shelf. Use brads to attach molding
to front edges of shelves.

3. Referring to Fig. 1, use screws to
assemble top, bottom, and two shutters
for cabinet frame.

Fig. 1

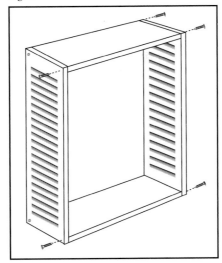

4. Cut hardboard to fit back of frame. Use
brads to attach back to frame.

5. Spacing "L" brackets evenly, refer to
Fig. 2 to attach brackets to inside of
cabinet for shelf supports.

Fig. 2

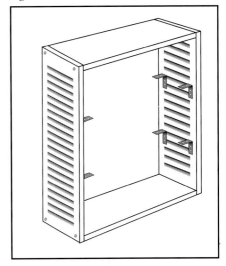

6. Use hinges to attach remaining shutters
to front of cabinet for doors.

7. Glue decorative brackets to top of
cabinet. Drive screws through inside of
cabinet into bottom of brackets to secure.

8. Apply primer and two coats of paint to
cabinet and shelves.

9. Place shelves in cabinet. Attach handles
to doors.

Elegant Faux Mantel

*F*eed the home fires with the warm look of this inviting faux mantel. Constructed from a castoff dresser hutch, the eye-catching piece sports decorative wood trim and marble-look veining. Use it anywhere you want to add an elegant touch — just fill the fireplace opening with plants, a screen, or art.

FIREPLACE FAÇADE

You will need a dresser hutch with mirror and shelves removed; saw; 1" x 12" lumber for backboard; decorative flat molding, wood glue; drill and countersink bit; wood screws; decorative wooden cutout; 3¹/₂"w fluted door molding; two 3¹/₂"w pieces of 7³/₄"w baseboard; finishing nails, bull-nose stair-step lumber; wood putty; sandpaper; tack cloth; white brush-on primer; paintbrushes; white, antique white, tan, brown, light grey, grey, dark grey, and black acrylic paint; natural sponge pieces; glazing medium; large feather; and glossy clear acrylic spray sealer.

Refer to Mantel Diagram to assemble mantel. Shaded areas indicate original hutch unit. Drill countersink pilot holes and fill with wood glue before driving screws to join surfaces unless otherwise indicated. To determine length of screws needed, measure thickness of

pieces to be joined and subtract ¹/₄". Allow glue, putty, primer, paint, and sealer to dry after each application.

1. Remove base from hutch. Measure inside width of hutch (A). For backboard, cut pieces of 1" x 12" lumber and decorative molding the determined measurement. Glue molding along one edge of backboard. With molding at bottom, attach backboard to hutch. Center and glue wooden cutout on backboard.

2. Measure from bottom of backboard to bottom edge of hutch (B); cut two pieces of fluted door molding the determined measurement. Use glue and finishing nails to attach molding, then baseboard pieces to hutch.

3. For mantel top, measure across top of hutch (C); add 3". Cut a piece of stair-step lumber the determined measurement; attach mantel top to hutch.

4. Cover heads of screws with wood putty. Sand mantel top, hutch, and base; wipe with tack cloth, then apply primer. Paint mantel top white, hutch antique white, and base black.

5. Follow *Sponge Painting*, page 124, to paint base with light grey, grey, then dark grey acrylic paint. Reattach base to hutch.

6. Using white, tan, and brown paint, follow *Marbling*, page 124, to paint mantel top.

7. Apply two coats of sealer to mantel.

MANTEL DIAGRAM

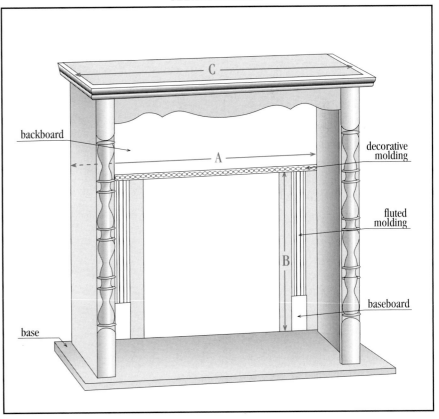

backboard

base

decorative molding

fluted molding

baseboard

AMAZING BOOK STAND

Compose this attractive book stand by turning the page on a flea market coffee table. "Edit" out its top and stand the base on end, then complete the amazing transformation with an antique-look silver finish.

TABLE LEG BOOK STAND

You will need a miter box and saw, 1½" dia. wooden spindle desired height for stand (we used the 31" spindle that was between the legs of our coffee table), drill and bits, two wooden "X"-shaped coffee table supports, four metal drawer pulls with decorative back plates for feet, 1"w decorative wooden molding, wood glue, small nails, 1" long wood screws, black spray paint, and metallic silver rub-on finish.

1. Cut one end of spindle at a 45° angle. Drill a pilot hole through center of each support and in each end of spindle.

2. For base of stand, drill a hole through end of each leg on one support. With back plates on top of base, attach drawer pulls to bottom of base for feet.

3. For top of stand, measure distance between ends of two legs on remaining support (Fig. 1). Cut a piece of molding the determined measurement. Glue, then nail molding to top of support for book rest; allow to dry.

Fig. 1

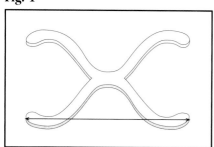

4. Use screws to attach base to flat end of spindle and top to angled end of spindle.

5. Paint book stand black. Follow manufacturer's instructions to apply rub-on finish to stand.

PAPERED IN ANIMAL PRINTS

Thinking of rescuing that shabby chest of drawers from the jungle of furnishings at the resale shop? Don't let its poor condition tame your creativity. Give it an exotic flair by dressing up the drawers with wallpaper in animal prints. Your family will be wild for it!

WALLPAPERED CHEST

You will need a wooden chest of drawers, painter's masking tape, primer, paintbrush, pre-pasted wallpaper in assorted animal prints, and decorative drawer pulls (optional).

1. Remove drawer pulls. Use tape to mask outer $1/4$" of each drawer front.

2. Apply primer to each drawer front; allow to dry. Remove tape.

3. Using a different print for each drawer, cut a piece of wallpaper to fit each primed area. Follow manufacturer's instructions to apply wallpaper to drawer fronts.

4. Replace drawer pulls with original or decorative pulls.

SNAPPY SUITCASE STORAGE

A generation ago, luggage was anything but light! Travelers today prefer featherweight nylon bags, but those old, heavy-duty suitcases are still serviceable as a decorative storage unit. Have fun picking out fabric for glue-in liners, and display the set proudly, stacked on a simple wooden stand.

SUITCASE STORAGE UNIT

You will need three hard-back suitcases in graduated sizes, fabric, spray adhesive, jute, hot glue gun, black spray paint, and a wooden luggage stand.

Refer to Suitcase Diagram for all measuring. Follow Steps 1 – 4 to line each suitcase.

1. Remove fabric lining from suitcase.

2. Measure length (A) and width (B) of lid; add $1/2$" to each measurement. Cut a piece from fabric the determined measurements. Apply spray adhesive to wrong side of fabric piece; clipping corners, smooth over inside of lid.

3. Measure around inside edge of lid (C), then measure depth of lid (D); add 1" to each measurement. Cut a strip from fabric the determined measurements. Press long edges and one end $1/2$" to wrong side. Apply spray adhesive to wrong side of strip. Beginning with raw end $1/2$" past one corner and matching one long edge to outer edge, adhere fabric strip to inner edges of lid.

4. Repeat Steps 2 and 3 to line bottom half of suitcase.

5. Wrap handles of suitcases with jute; hot glue ends to secure.

6. Paint stand black; allow to dry. Arrange suitcases on stand.

SUITCASE DIAGRAM

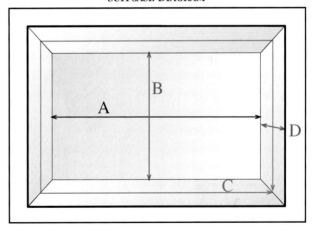

DRYING-RACK ACCENT TABLE

Furnishing a new home or apartment can be expensive. But shoppers who are budget-conscious know that flea markets are fabulous places for discovering great finds. Topped with glass, a foldaway wooden clothes-drying rack makes a quaint little accent table. Bundles of dried flowers, hanging from the slats, give cottage-garden charm to the table.

CLOTHES RACK ENTRY TABLE

You will need a saw, folding wooden clothes-drying rack, wood glue, small brads, 8' lattice strip, raffia, dried flowers, clear self-adhesive surface protectors, and a glass to fit tabletop (we used a $19^{1}/_{2}$" x $33^{1}/_{2}$" piece of glass).

Allow wood glue to dry after each application.

1. Referring to Fig. 1, cut top from rack, then cut dowels and six 1" spacers from top.

Fig. 1

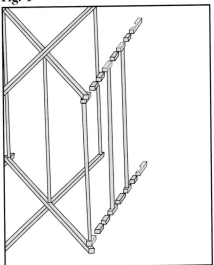

2. Expand rack to desired size for table; glue joints to secure.

3. Glue a spacer to each end of one dowel. Referring to Fig. 2, glue dowels and spacers to rack; use brads to secure.

Fig. 2

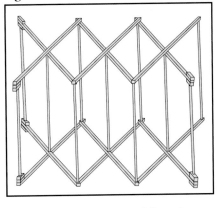

4. Cut lattice strip into two 4-foot pieces. Referring to Fig. 3, use brads to attach lattice strips across back of rack for supports; trim ends if necessary.

Fig. 3

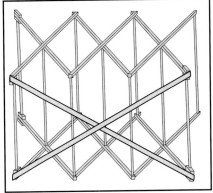

5. Use raffia to hang dried flower bundles from top of rack.

6. To complete table, adhere surface protectors to top of rack; place glass on table.

COUNTRY STOOL

You'll have no trouble ruling the roost after making this padded stool! Remove the back from a mismatched dining chair and cover the seat with foam and decorative fabric. Paint the legs with a trio of colors, then lightly sand to achieve a rustic look that's definitely something to crow about!

PADDED STOOL

You will need a saw, wooden chair, sandpaper, tack cloth, spray primer, assorted colors of acrylic paint to coordinate with fabric (we used red, brown, and tan), paintbrushes, clear acrylic spray sealer, 2" thick foam, cotton batting, fabric, staple gun, hot glue gun, and ³/₄"w gimp trim.

Painting instructions indicate the colors we used; substitute paint colors to coordinate with your fabric as desired. Allow primer, paint, and sealer to dry after each application.

1. For stool, cut back from chair even with seat. Sand stool; wipe with tack cloth.

2. Apply primer, then two coats of tan paint to stool. Follow *Dry Brush*, page 123, to paint stool with brown paint. Apply a light coat of red paint to stool. Lightly sand stool; wipe with tack cloth.

3. Apply two coats of sealer to stool.

4. For cushion, draw around seat on foam, batting, and wrong side of fabric. Cut out foam along drawn line. Cut out batting and fabric 3" outside drawn line.

5. Place fabric right side down on a flat surface. Place batting on fabric, then center foam and stool on batting. Fold edges of fabric to bottom of seat and staple in place. Gather corners and staple in place; trim excess fabric at corners even with bottom edge of seat.

6. Overlapping ends at back and covering raw edges of fabric and staples at corners, glue trim along bottom edge of seat.

FIREPLACE ORGANIZER

When cold weather starts creeping in, you'll be glad you have this handy organizer filled with everything you need to build a crackling fire. Just remove the legs from an old tiered accent table and stand the table up on its end. The "pocket" between the tiers keeps dried kindling accessible, and a galvanized bucket tucks in nicely to hold fireplace tools. A flattened metal can forms a hanging matchbox.

FIREPLACE ORGANIZER

Tool Bucket

You will need a metal bucket; light brown, brown, and rust acrylic paint; foam brush; and natural sponge pieces.

1. Paint bucket brown; allow to dry.

2. *Sponge Paint*, page 124, bucket light brown, then rust; allow to dry.

Match Holder

You will need a metal can; hammer and large nail; light brown, brown, and rust acrylic paint; foam brush; natural sponge pieces; black craft wire; and wire cutters.

1. Remove both ends from can. With seam of can at center back, flatten bottom of can and shape top into a narrow oval.

2. Use hammer and nail to punch holes along bottom edge of can and to punch a hole at each side of top.

3. Paint can brown; allow to dry.

4. *Sponge Paint*, page 124, can light brown, then rust; allow to dry.

5. Lace wire through holes along bottom of can; trim ends. Wrap center of a 15" length of wire around a pencil several times to form hanger. Wrap ends of hanger through holes on sides of can.

Wood Box

You will need a wooden end table with shelf and upholstery tacks.

1. Remove legs from table. Turn table upright on end.

2. Use tack to attach Match Holder to box. Place Tool Bucket in box.

SUNNY PLANT TABLE

Pamper your plants while creating an attractive coffee table for yourself. The pretty plant stand is made from an upturned end table, a transformed top, and an under-cabinet fluorescent light. Add a sunny coat of paint, and your flowers will be blooming in no time!

PLANT LIGHT TABLE

You will need a wooden end table, saw, $1/2$" hardboard, 1" long wood screws, miter box and saw, $2^1/2$"w wooden molding, 1" long nails, wood putty, sandpaper, tack cloth, spray primer, acrylic paint, paintbrush, matte clear acrylic spray sealer, and a self-adhesive battery-operated fluorescent light.

Allow wood putty, primer, paint, and sealer to dry after each application.

1. Remove top from table; set aside.

2. Draw around table bottom on smooth side of hardboard (Fig. 1); cut out just inside drawn lines. Use screws to attach hardboard piece to table bottom.

Fig. 1

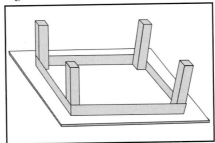

3. Place tabletop on legs of table bottom. Countersinking screws, use screws to attach top to legs.

4. For trim, measure edges of tabletop. Mitering corners, cut lengths of molding the determined measurements. Use nails to attach trim to edges of tabletop. (*If your tabletop has rounded corners, you can nail flexible resin trim along the entire edge.*)

5. Fill holes or gaps with wood putty. Sand table; wipe with tack cloth. Apply primer, paint, then two coats of sealer to table.

6. Follow manufacturer's instructions to attach light to underside of tabletop.

BOUNTIFUL BIRDBATH TABLE

*C*apture a bit of nature in the blink of an eye with this glass-topped birdbath table! Brush on woodland hues with sage acrylic paint, and fill the basin with moss, bark, antique bird prints, feathers, a bird nest, and other backyard finds. Family and guests will appreciate these reminders of the world's simple wonders.

BIRDBATH TABLE

You will need heavy-duty sandpaper, concrete birdbath, tack cloth, green acrylic paint, paintbrush, clear acrylic spray sealer, items to display in birdbath (we used dried sheet moss, bark pieces, dried fern fronds, bird prints found at a flea market, dried flowers, rocks, feathers, and a bird's nest with eggs), clear self-adhesive surface protectors, and a piece of tempered glass for tabletop.

Allow paint and sealer to dry after each application.

1. Sand birdbath; wipe with tack cloth.

2. Follow *Dry Brush*, page 123, to apply green paint to birdbath. Apply two coats of sealer to birdbath.

3. Arrange display items in birdbath as desired.

4. Adhere surface protectors along top edge of birdbath; place glass on table.

WHIMSICAL WALLPAPER TABLE

*R*escue a discarded cabinet door to make this charming glass-topped accent table. Let your imagination guide your choice of scenic wallpaper for the top, then decorate the edge with a painted border and use stepladders for legs. You'll have a table that will add life to any room!

LADDER TABLE

You will need a wooden cabinet door; wood putty; sandpaper; two wooden two-step ladders the same height; tack cloth; white spray primer; cream and tan acrylic paint; desired colors of acrylic paint to coordinate with wallpaper; paintbrushes; pre-pasted wallpaper; clear self-adhesive surface protectors; and tempered glass to fit tabletop.

Allow wood putty, primer, paint, and sealer to dry after each application.

1. Remove hardware and knobs from door; fill holes with wood putty. Sand door and ladders; wipe with tack cloth.

2. Apply primer to door. Follow *Dry Brush*, page 123, to paint ladders tan, then cream.

3. Paint frame of door cream. Paint designs along frame to match designs in wallpaper.

4. Cut a piece from wallpaper to fit in center of door; follow manufacturer's instructions to secure wallpaper in place.

5. Adhere surface protectors to corners of door. Place tabletop across ladders, then place glass on tabletop.

POETIC WRITING DESK

The secret to composing this poetic writing desk is using its top drawer to create a handy bookcase and applying sheer fabric to dress up the drop leaf. To preserve its old-fashioned character, the secondhand secretary was painted ivory and then sanded for an aged look. Wicker baskets replace the missing drawer, and decorative screen-door brackets provide creative flair. A plush tassel and drawer pulls resembling antique keys add distinction.

SECRETARY

You will need a wooden secretary with drawers, drill and bits, wood screws, four decorative wooden brackets, plywood, wood putty, sandpaper, tack cloth, brown primer, paste floor wax, ivory acrylic paint, paintbrushes, sheer print fabric, decoupage glue, foam brushes, clear acrylic brush-on sealer, and replacement drawer pulls (optional).

To determine length of wood screws needed, measure thickness of pieces to be joined and subtract $1/4$". Drill pilot holes before inserting screws into wood; countersink all screws.

1. For hutch, remove top drawer from secretary; remove pulls from drawer. Center drawer on top of secretary along back edge; use screws to attach in place.

2. Use screws to attach wooden brackets to inside top corners of hutch and to bottom of secretary.

3. For hutch shelf, measure inside depth and width of hutch; cut a piece from plywood the determined measurements. Use screws to attach shelf in hutch.

4. Use wood putty to fill in holes and cover screw heads; allow to dry. Sand secretary; wipe with tack cloth.

5. Apply primer, then a light coat of wax to secretary. Paint secretary ivory; lightly sand for an aged look; wipe with tack cloth.

6. Measure length and width of drop front on secretary; add 2" to each measurement. Cut a piece from fabric the determined measurement.

7. Apply a thin layer of glue to drop front. Center fabric on front and smooth in place; apply glue over fabric. Allow to dry. Trim edges of fabric even with edges of front.

8. Apply two coats of sealer to secretary.

9. Replace pulls on secretary.

GRAND SLAM BED

Little boys love old sports paraphernalia, and where better to find sought-after gear than secondhand shops. An outdated headboard becomes a winning asset when painted in uniform stripes and embellished with wooden stars and baseball finials. Accented by a pair of crisscrossed bats, the footboard scores a home run, and the price for this designer look is definitely in the ballpark!

BASEBALL BED FRAME

You will need sandpaper; wooden headboard and footboard; tack cloth; spray primer; cream, red, and blue acrylic paint; paintbrushes; three wooden star cutouts; 1"w painter's masking tape; drill and bits; two baseballs; two double-ended screws; wood glue; two wooden baseball bats; miter box and saw; hot glue gun; wood screws; and clear acrylic spray sealer.

To determine length of wood screws needed, measure thickness of footboard and add 1". Allow primer, paint, and sealer to dry after each application.

1. Sand headboard and footboard; wipe with tack cloth.

2. Apply primer to headboard and footboard, then paint center sections cream; paint posts and stars red. Lightly sand edges of stars and wipe with tack cloth.

3. Beginning at center and working outward and spacing tape strips $1/4$" apart, mask stripes down cream sections of headboard and footboard. Paint stripes blue, then remove tape.

4. For finials, drill holes slightly smaller than double-ended screws in each baseball and at center of each headboard post. Fill holes with wood glue, then use double-ended screws to attach balls to posts. Use wood glue to attach stars to headboard; allow to dry.

5. Mark one bat 10" from handle end. Using miter box, cut bat at a 30° angle at mark. Using hot glue, arrange and spot glue bats on footboard in an "X" shape. Working from back side of footboard, use wood screws to secure bats in place.

6. Apply sealer to headboard and footboard.

"FABRIC-ATED" STAND

Painting isn't the only way to breathe new life into battered furnishings. Try dressing pieces in fabric for a bold, colorful look. We transformed a bedside nightstand into a crafter's table simply by gluing assorted fabrics onto the stand. What a fun way to coordinate furnishings!

NIGHTSTAND ORGANIZER

You will need ¹/₄" plywood (optional), wooden nightstand, sandpaper, tack cloth, primer, acrylic paint, paintbrushes, clear acrylic sealer, coordinating fabrics, decoupage glue, and pinking shears.

1. If necessary, cut a piece from plywood to fit in nightstand for shelf.

2. Sand stand; wipe with tack cloth. Apply primer, paint, then sealer to top and any beveled edges that would be difficult to cover with fabric; allow to dry.

3. *If your stand has curved edges, trim the fabric 1" past the curved edge, clip the curves, and smooth the fabric around the edges.* Cutting fabric pieces ¹/₄" larger to wrap around exterior front and back edges, cut pieces from desired fabrics to fit surfaces to be covered. Use decoupage glue to adhere fabric pieces in place. Use pinking shears to cut strips from fabric to fit along front facings of stand; use decoupage glue to adhere in place. Allow to dry.

HOME ENTERTAINMENT CENTER

You don't have to pay a fortune to find an entertainment center that matches your décor. Just buy an inexpensive chest of drawers at the flea market, then "tune in" a new look with fresh paint and woven rattan fabric. Slide your VCR in one of the empty shelves, place baskets for videos in the other, and sit back and enjoy the show!

ENTERTAINMENT CABINET

You will need a wooden chest of drawers, saw, $^3/_8$" plywood, 2" long "L" brackets and wood screws (optional), 1" x 2" lumber, wood screws, putty, sandpaper, tack cloth, black acrylic paint, paintbrushes, acrylic paint to coordinate with fabric, woven rattan fabric, staple gun, thick craft glue, and replacement drawer pulls (optional).

To determine length of wood screws needed, measure thickness of pieces to be joined and subtract $^1/_4$". Drill pilot holes before inserting screws into wood.

1. Remove drawers from chest. For each shelf, cut a piece of plywood to fit in opening. If necessary, attach "L" brackets to sides and back of chest for shelf supports. Place shelves in chest.

2. Sand chest; wipe with tack cloth. Apply primer to chest. Paint inside of chest black; allow to dry. Paint outside of chest with coordinating paint; allow to dry.

3. Remove pulls from drawers. To cover each drawer front, measure length and width of drawer front; add 2" to each measurement. Cut a piece from fabric the determined measurements.

4. Place fabric wrong side up on a flat surface; center drawer front on fabric. Pulling fabric taut and folding at corners, wrap fabric to back of drawer front. If necessary, trim edges of fabric. Apply glue along edges of fabric to prevent fraying; allow to dry.

5. Measure length and width of side areas of chest to be covered; cut pieces from fabric the determined measurements. Glue fabric pieces to sides of chest; allow to dry.

6. Replace drawer pulls on chest.

SODA CRATE CHEST

*B*ack in the days when soda pop came in glass bottles, wooden crates were handy to have. You can make them just as useful today as drawers in this innovative caddy! Assemble a chest from pieces of plywood, then paint and sand it to create an antique appearance. Simply slide in the "crate" drawers, and enjoy your new furniture accent.

SODA CRATE CHEST

You will need a saw, 4' x 8' sheet of 3/4" plywood, sandpaper, tack cloth, wood glue, drill with regular and countersink bits, 1 1/2" long wood screws, 3/4"w molding, 1" long finishing nails, miter box with saw, wood putty, red acrylic paint, paintbrushes, clear acrylic spray sealer, dowel to fit in holes of spools, five wooden thread spools, five wooden soft drink crates, household cement, and five metal bottle caps.

Apply wood glue to each surface to be joined. Drill countersink pilot holes and fill with wood glue before driving screws to join surfaces together.

1. Refer to Cutting Diagram, page 127, to cut chest pieces from plywood; sand rough edges and wipe with tack cloth.

2. Referring to Assembly Diagram, attach bottom, bottom facings, top facings, then bottom shelf to sides. Measuring from top of bottom shelf, mark interior of sides at 5" intervals for shelf placement. Place chest on back. With top of each shelf aligned with marks, use screws to secure shelves in chest.

3. Attach back to chest. Matching back edges, center top on chest. Use screws to attach top to chest.

4. Cut two 31" and six 19" lengths of molding. Matching interior edge of chest to edge of molding; glue, then nail 31" lengths of molding down front of chest. Matching top edge of shelf with edge of molding; glue, then nail 19" lengths of molding along shelves and bottom of chest.

5. Mitering front corners, cut molding to fit front and side edges of top; glue, then nail in place.

6. Apply wood putty over screw and nail heads; allow to dry. Sand chest; wipe with tack cloth.

7. Paint chest and allow to dry.

8. Apply two coats of sealer to chest; allow to dry.

9. For each drawer pull, cut a 1" length of dowel. Glue 1/2" of dowel piece in hole of spool. Drill a hole, same size as dowel at center on one long side of crate. Glue dowel on spool in hole in crate. Use household cement to glue a bottle cap to end of spool. Place drawers in chest.

ASSEMBLY DIAGRAM

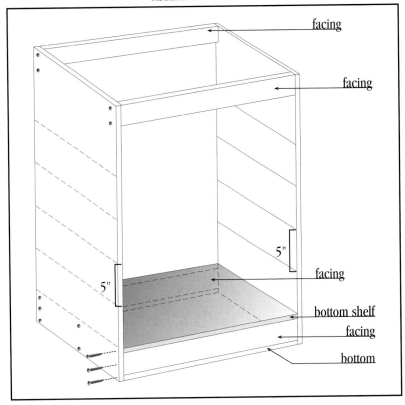

facing

facing

5"

5"

facing

bottom shelf

facing

bottom

LICENSE PLATE HEADBOARD

*D**riven to collect old license plates during your flea market junkets? Then turn the fruits of your travels into a headboard that logs your various journeys. The plates are simply attached with wood screws to a piece of painted hardboard. What a great way to rev up a teenager's room!*

LICENSE PLATE HEADBOARD

For a twin-size headboard, you will need a 36" x 42" piece of ¼" hardboard, two 42" long pieces of 1" x 6" lumber, eight 1" long wood screws, black spray paint, 21 license plates, and eighty-four ³/₈" long wood screws.

1. To assemble headboard, use 1" screws to attach 1" x 6" legs to back of hardboard (Fig. 1).

Fig. 1

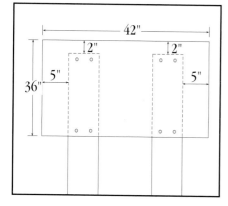

2. Paint headboard black; allow to dry.

3. Arrange license plates on headboard. Use ³/₈" screws to attach plates to headboard.

"WHEELY NEAT" NIGHTSTAND

Any automobile enthusiast will love the "engine-uity" of this bedside table fashioned from well-traveled wheel rims. Stacked in alternating sizes, the rims sport an array of colorful paints suggestive of racing flags — and they're primed for endurance! Add a glass top, and you're guaranteed a winning finish.

WHEEL NIGHTSTAND

You will need a stiff scrub brush; two 12" dia. and three 13" dia. wheels; spray primer; spray paint to paint wheels (we used yellow, red, blue, green, and black); silver spray paint; hot glue gun; and a 20" dia. tempered-glass tabletop.

Allow primer and paint to dry after each application.

1. Scrub wheels thoroughly with hot soapy water; rinse and allow to dry.

2. Apply primer, then two coats of desired color of paint to each wheel. Paint center of one 13" dia. wheel silver.

3. Beginning with a 13" dia. wheel and alternating sizes, stack wheels with silver wheel on top. Run a line of hot glue along top edge of nightstand; allow to harden. Place glass on nightstand.

GENERAL INSTRUCTIONS

ADHESIVES

When using any adhesive, carefully follow the manufacturer's instructions.

White Craft Glue: Recommended for paper. Dry flat.

Tacky Craft Glue: Recommended for paper, fabric, florals, or wood. Dry flat or secure items with clothespins or straight pins until glue is dry.

Craft Glue Stick: Recommended for paper or for gluing small, lightweight items to paper or other surface. Dry flat.

Fabric Glue: Recommended for fabric or paper. Dry flat or secure items with clothespins or straight pins until glue is dry.

Decoupage Glue: Recommended for decoupaging fabric or paper to a surface such as wood or glass. Use purchased decoupage glue or mix one part craft glue with one part water.

Hot or Low-Temperature Glue Gun: Recommended for paper, fabric, florals, or wood. Hold in place until set.

Rubber Cement: Recommended for paper or cardboard. May discolor photos; may discolor paper with age. Dry flat (dries very quickly).

Spray Adhesive: Recommended for adhering two surfaces together; exposed surfaces will remain tacky. Can be repositionable or permanent.

Household Cement: Recommended for ceramic or metal. Secure items with clothespins until glue is dry.

Wood Glue: Recommended for wood. Unless item is nailed or screwed together, clamp until glue is dry.

CUTTING A FABRIC CIRCLE

1. Cut a square of fabric the size indicated in project instructions.

2. Matching right sides, fold fabric square in half from top to bottom and again from left to right.

3. Tie one end of string to a pencil or fabric marking pen. Measuring from pencil, insert a thumbtack through string at length indicated in project instructions. Insert thumbtack through folded corner of fabric. Holding tack in place and keeping string taut, mark cutting line (Fig. 1).

Fig. 1

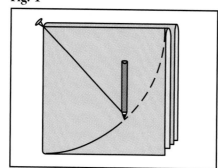

4. Cut along drawn line through all fabric layers.

DECOUPAGE

1. Cut desired motifs from fabric or paper.

2. Apply decoupage glue to wrong sides of motifs.

3. Arrange motifs on project as desired, overlapping as necessary. Smooth in place and allow to dry.

4. Apply two to three coats of sealer to project, allowing to dry after each application.

EMBROIDERY STITCHES
Cross Stitch

Bring needle up at 1 and go down at 2. Come up at 3 and go down at 4 (Fig. 1).

Fig. 1

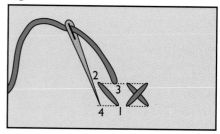

Running Stitch

Referring to Fig. 2, make a series of straight stitches with stitch length equal to the space between stitches.

Fig. 2

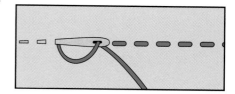

BOWS

Loop sizes given in project instructions refer to the length of ribbon used to make one loop of bow. If no size is given, make loops desired size for project.

1. For first streamer, measure desired length of streamer from one end of ribbon; twist ribbon between fingers (Fig. 1).

Fig. 1

2. Keeping right side of ribbon facing out, fold ribbon to front to form desired-size loop; gather ribbon between fingers (Fig. 2). Fold ribbon to back to form another loop; gather ribbon between fingers (Fig. 3).

Fig. 2

Fig. 3

3. *If a center loop is desired, form half the desired number of loops, then loosely wrap ribbon around thumb and gather ribbon between fingers as shown in Fig. 4; form remaining loops.* Continue to form loops, varying size of loops as desired, until bow is desired size.

Fig. 4

4. For remaining streamer, trim ribbon to desired length.

5. To secure bow, hold gathered loops tightly. Fold a length of floral wire around gathers of loops. Hold wire ends behind bow, gathering all loops forward; twist bow to tighten wire. Arrange loops and trim ribbon ends as desired.

PAINTING TECHNIQUES

To achieve the desired results, practice these decorative painting basics before beginning project.

Preparing Project for Painting:

Remove any hardware and set aside. If necessary, repair any holes, cracks, or other imperfections. Sand item and wipe with tack cloth. Apply primer and allow to dry. Paint project according to instructions. Clean and reattach hardware or replace with new hardware.

Transferring Patterns:

Trace pattern onto tracing paper. Using removable tape, tape pattern to project. Place transfer paper, coated-side down, between project and traced pattern. Use a stylus to transfer outlines of design to project. If necessary, use a soft eraser to remove any smudges.

Painting Basecoats:

A foam plate makes a good palette. Select a paintbrush according to project size: for example, when painting a large item, use a large flat brush; when painting a small item, select a small brush. Several coats may be necessary for even coverage. Allow paint to dry after each coat.

Painting Dots:

Dip the tip of a round paintbrush, the handle end of a paintbrush, the new eraser on a pencil, or one end of a toothpick in paint and touch to project; dip in paint each time for uniform dots.

Dry Brush:

Do not dip brush in water. Dip a stipple brush or an old paintbrush in paint; wipe most of the paint off onto a dry paper towel. Using tips of bristles, lightly brush over the surface of the project; decrease pressure on the brush as you move outward. Repeat until desired effect is achieved.

Linework:

Thin paint to an ink-like consistency. Dip brush in water; blot on paper towel. Load brush by placing bristles in paint and dragging away from paint to get a pointed tip. Place tip on surface and pull brush toward you.

Marbling:

1. Using colors of paint specified in project instructions, mix three separate glazes (a light, a medium, and a dark color). Make each glaze by mixing two parts clear glazing medium with one part paint on a foam plate.

2. For veining, use a pencil to lightly draw main veins diagonally across surface; draw short, thin branches of veins coming off main veins.

3. *Work in small sections while glaze is still wet to blend colors.* Brush white glaze over veins in one section. Lightly *Sponge Paint* over section with medium glaze, blending colors to achieve desired effect.

4. Using a feather or a liner brush dipped in dark glaze, drag it over the veins, wiggling and flipping feather in a random or irregular movement.

5. Use a dampened sponge to blend paints so no harsh lines are visible.

6. Dampen feather, then drag tips through white glaze mixture. Brush tips back and forth over entire surface to mute and blend colors together; allow to dry. Apply two to three coats of sealer to surface; allow to dry.

Side-Loading for Shading or Highlighting:

Dip one corner of a flat brush in water; blot on paper towel. Dip dry corner of brush into paint. Stroke brush back and forth on palette until there is a gradual change from paint to water in each brush stroke. Stroke loaded side of brush along detail line on project, pulling brush toward you and turning project, if necessary.

For Shading, side-load brush with a darker color of paint.

For Highlighting, side-load brush with a lighter color of paint.

Sponge Painting:

Use an assembly line method when making several projects; practice technique on scrap paper until desired look is achieved.

Place project on a covered work surface. Paint project with first color and allow to dry before moving to next color.

To *Sponge Paint* surface, use a pouncing or stamping motion, changing the direction of the sponge every few presses and slightly overlapping areas. Reapplying paint to sponge as necessary, fill any missed areas, but still allow the basecoat color to show through. Rinse sponge before using next color.

For allover designs, dip a dampened sponge piece into paint; blot on a paper towel to remove excess paint. *Sponge Paint* project.

For painting with sponge shapes, dip a dampened sponge shape into paint; blot on a paper towel to remove excess paint. Lightly press sponge onto project; carefully lift sponge. Allow to dry. Repeat to paint additional shapes on project.

Stenciling:

1. To make stencil, cut a piece of template plastic at least 1" larger on all sides than pattern. Place template plastic directly over pattern in book. Use a fine-point permanent marker to trace over lines of pattern. Place template plastic on cutting mat and use craft knife to cut out design sections, making sure edges are smooth.

2. Pour a small amount of paint onto a foam plate. Hold or tape (using removable tape) stencil in place on project. Dip a stencil brush or sponge piece in paint and remove excess on a paper towel. Working from edges of cut out areas toward center, apply paint in a stamping motion. Carefully lift stencil from project. To stencil a design in reverse, clean stencil and turn stencil over.

BINDING

1. Cut a $2^1/_4$"w fabric strip 1" longer than each edge to be bound. Press one long edge of strip $^1/_2$" to wrong side.

2. Matching raw edges and right side of binding to wrong side of project piece, use a $^1/_2$" seam allowance to sew binding to bottom edge of piece. Fold pressed edge to right side, covering stitching; topstitch in place. Trim binding ends even with raw edges.

3. Matching raw edges, right side of binding to wrong side of project piece, and extending binding $^1/_2$" past bottom edge, sew binding to each side edge. For each side, fold bottom end of binding $^1/_2$" to wrong side, then fold long edge to right side, covering stitching; topstitch in place. Trim binding even with top edge of piece.

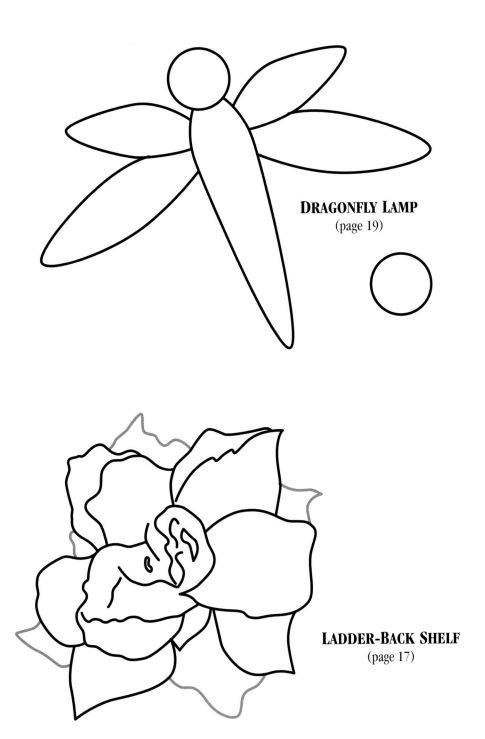

DRAGONFLY LAMP
(page 19)

LADDER-BACK SHELF
(page 17)

CUTTING DIAGRAM

Side 12" x 31"	Side 12" x 31"	Back 20" x 31"
Shelf 12" x 19"	Shelf 12" x 19"	Shelf 12" x 19"	Top 13" x 22"
Shelf 12" x 19"	Shelf 12" x 19"	Bottom 12" x 19"	
Facing 2½" x 19"	Facing 2½" x 19"		
Facing 2½" x 19"	Facing 2½" x 19"		

4'

8'

SODA CRATE CHEST
(page 118)

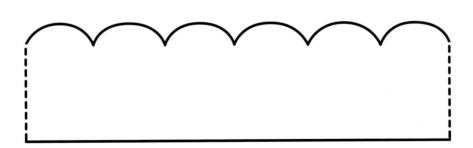

CHICKEN-FEEDER CANDLEHOLDER
(page 48)

CREDITS

We want to extend a warm *thank you* to the generous people who allowed us to photograph our projects at their homes: Dan and Sandra Cook, Anne Jarrard, Tim and Janna Laughlin, Ellison Poe, Duncan Nancy Porter, Catherine Smith, and Patricia A. Sowers.

To Wisconsin Technicolor LLC of Pewaukee, Wisconsin, we say *thank you* for the superb color reproduction and excellent pre-press preparation.

We want to especially thank photographers Andrew Uilkie and Ken West of Peerless Photography, and Jerry R. Davis of Jerry Davis Photography, all of Little Rock, Arkansas, for their time, patience, and excellent work. Photography stylists Sondra Daniel and Jan Nobles also deserve a special mention for the high quality of their collaboration with these photographers.

We would like to recognize Viking Husqvarna Sewing Machine Company of Cleveland, Ohio, for providing the sewing machines used to make many of our projects.

We also want to thank Nancy Porter for providing the props used in the *Bountiful Birdbath Table*, page 110.

We bestow a special word of thanks to Rosetta Riendeau who designed the *Kitchen Towel Tree* on page 84.